ON RELIGION

ON RELIGION

The Revelation of God as the Sublimation of Religion

Karl Barth

Translated and Introduced by Garrett Green

t&t clark

Published by T&T Clark
A Continuum imprint
The Tower Building, 11 York Road, London SE1 7NX
80 Maiden Lane, Suite 704, New York, NY 10038

www.tandtclark.com

British Library Cataloguing-in-Publication Data
A catalogue record for this book is available from the British Library

Typeset by Fakenham Photosetting Limited, Fakenham, Norfolk
Printed and bound in Great Britain by Cromwell Press Ltd, Trowbridge, Wiltshire

ISBN 056703108X (hardback)
ISBN 0567031098 (paperback)

CONTENTS

TRANSLATOR'S PREFACE   vii

INTRODUCTION: BARTH AS THEORIST OF RELIGION   1

THE REVELATION OF GOD AS THE SUBLIMATION OF
RELIGION   33
1. The Problem of Religion in Theology   33
2. Religion as Faithlessness   53
3. The True Religion   85

Notes   127
Select Bibliography   139

Translator's Preface

Garrett Green

It is generally acknowledged that translation is as much an art as a science, requiring not only linguistic expertise in two languages but also a sense of style and tone in both. Any translator, therefore – especially one who is translating a text that has been translated before – owes the reader some accounting of his own presuppositions and approach, including his reasons for retranslating an already published work. The original translators of Barth's *Church Dogmatics* rendered an invaluable service, and every reader of Barth in English owes them a debt of gratitude for their Herculean efforts. For over half a century scholars and students have been the beneficiaries of their work. The English translation of the *Church Dogmatics* appeared in a series of publications by T&T Clark Ltd., Edinburgh, starting with the first half-volume in 1936 (designated I/1) and continuing until the final fragmentary part of Barth's unfinished volume 4 (designated IV/4) appeared in 1969. The Index Volume completed the English edition in 1977. Under the general editorship of G. W. Bromiley and T. F. Torrance, the *Church Dogmatics* was the work of a number of translators. Maintaining consistency in a project carried out over so many years by a variety of translators was not always possible, a fact acknowledged by the editors in 1975 when they brought out Bromiley's new translation of vol. I/1, originally the sole work of G. T. Thomson. Thomson had also managed a partial translation of vol. I/2, which includes the section contained in the present volume, before declining health forced his retirement from the project. Harold Knight revised and completed Thomson's work and published the second part-volume in 1956.

No translation is flawless, and as Barth studies have developed and become more sophisticated, the need for revision or retranslation into English has become increasingly evident. Some of the more important reasons include the following:

1. The original translation contains a number of errors, including not only occasional mistranslations but a few cases in which entire sentences, or parts of sentences, have been omitted. In addition, the choice of words in English often does not capture Barth's meaning as accurately, or as gracefully, as it might. Though I have undoubtedly made some errors of my

own, I believe that this new translation improves the accuracy and precision of the English, while rendering Barth's prose in an English style more in keeping with his own style in German.

2. Barth makes frequent use of a typographical convention not employed in English: what the Germans call *gesperrte Schrift*, in which extra spaces are inserted between the letters of certain words to indicate emphasis. The equivalent in English would be the use of italics. Barth's original translators made the unfortunate decision simply to ignore these emphasized words and phrases in most cases. The problem is that Barth makes frequent use of emphasis in sometimes subtle but significant ways; for example, he will repeat a phrase or sentence verbatim, stressing one word the first time and another the second. I have restored Barth's emphasis, usually through the use of italics but occasionally by other means (e.g., through word order or the use of intensifying modifiers).

3. When Barth cites scripture, he generally translates the Hebrew or Greek text into German himself, though in the case of New Testament passages he often cites the original Greek without translating it. In place of Barth's own translations into contemporary German, the translators of the *Church Dogmatics* used the Authorized (King James) version, which lends Barth's English an archaically pious tone quite out of keeping with the German original. Over the decades since Barth wrote, that classic version of the English Bible has become increasingly unfamiliar, even to church-going speakers of English. I have therefore employed the Revised Standard Version in most cases, which I believe to be the clearest and most straightforward of the many contemporary English translations, and the one that does the best job of staying as close as possible to the original. I have changed the English of the RSV only in cases required by Barth's diction in referring to the passage. In the cases where Barth cites the New Testament in Greek, the original English translators did the same; but in these situations I have substituted English translations based on the RSV. This change is necessitated by the fact that even many theological students and clergy – not to mention the general reader, for whom this new translation is particularly intended – no longer learn the biblical languages well enough to read them.

4. By far the most important reason for retranslating §17 of the *Church Dogmatics* is, however, an egregious error in the title and leading concept of the section. The translation of the title – 'The Revelation of God as the Abolition of Religion' – has left generations of English readers with the false impression that Barth thinks revelation simply replaces religion with something else. Not a few theologically educated English speakers hold the utterly erroneous belief that Karl Barth does not think that Christianity is a religion at all! Just a glance at the title of the third and final subsection – 'True Religion' – ought to have disabused them of this misconception (though this title too was inaccurately rendered in the old translation, since

Barth clearly intends the final section to be about '*The* True Religion', namely, the Christian religion). One ought not judge the translators of the *Church Dogmatics* too harshly, however, for the term *Aufhebung* (which they translated as 'abolition') confronts any translator with a dilemma, since no one English word can reproduce the unique ambiguity of the German term. (For the history, significance, and meaning of the term, see the discussion in the Introduction, pp. 5–6 below.) One possibility would be to follow the practice of the translators of Hegel's *Lectures on the Philosophy of Religion* by employing the etymologically equivalent terms 'sublate' and 'sublation'.[1] The chief drawback of this solution is that *aufheben* is a common verb in everyday German, whereas the reader in English doesn't know what to make of the odd term 'sublation'. The other available alternative is to render *Aufhebung* as 'sublimation', a word that actually occurs in English and shares a similar etymology. The main drawback is that 'sublimation' is familiar as a technical term in the translations of Sigmund Freud's psycho-analytic writings. Barth's term, of course, has nothing whatever to do with this Freudian concept (Freud's term is not *Aufhebung* but *Sublimierung*); so if 'sublimation' is to be employed as the translation of *Aufhebung* – as it is in the present translation – readers need to be forewarned of this possible confusion. The strongest reason for choosing 'sublimation' is its close kinship to the English term 'sublime', whose connotations do a better job of suggesting Barth's meaning. To sublimate something – i.e., to make it sublime – suggests that it will become both higher and better as a result. To these native associations of the English word 'sublimation', the reader must then add the dialectical pole of negation in order properly to grasp Barth's meaning.

Something should be said about the issue of 'gendered language', which unavoidably confronts any translator of texts written before about 1970, when it became a virtual dogma in academia that the so-called generic use of grammatically masculine terminology to refer to human beings collectively or in general was forbidden. At the risk of having Barth's text dismissed for ideological reasons, I have decided to retain his masculine language and imagery. Several points need to be made in defence of this practice:

1. Historical accuracy forbids the translator from altering a text from an earlier generation in order to make it more palatable to contemporary readers. A useful test in such cases is to ask what an educated speaker of English, of approximately the same background and occupation as Karl Barth, would have said at that time when expressing similar ideas in English. The answer is obvious: when we consult theological works of the 1930s we find frequent, unselfconscious use of such phrases as 'God and man', 'mankind', etc. Even more obviously, 'God' invariably takes masculine pronouns. To force the Barth of 1930s to speak twenty-first-century politically-correct English would violate the integrity of the text.

It would also patronize readers by implying that they cannot be trusted to arrive at their own interpretation of the text. Whether or not Barth should be criticized for sexist language or any other alleged failing is a question best left to the judgment of readers and not preempted by the translator.

2. Even if it were desirable on ideological grounds to use 'gender-neutral' language in translating Barth's German, it would introduce an unacceptable degree of ambiguity and wordiness into the text. So frequent are the masculine pronouns for both humanity and divinity, that the substitution of dualities such as 'his or her' (not to mention the unsightly and unpronounceable 'he/she' and 'his/hers') would make Barth's text so verbose and confusing that it would become difficult for the reader to follow the grammatical and syntactical connections.

3. One should also remember that Barth sounds more 'gender specific' in English than in German, since 'man' in the English translation almost always renders the German *Mensch*, a word that is masculine in grammar but not in meaning (it denotes the human being, including both sexes). For today's reader this problem is exacerbated by the nearly total disappearance in English usage of the important distinction between gender and sex. (Nowadays one can be asked to fill out forms requesting one's 'gender', though most people will still answer by using the adjectives of sexuality, 'male' or 'female', rather than those of gender, 'masculine' or 'feminine'.)

4. Not only the clarity but also the content of Barth's theology would be altered by eliminating gendered language. Barth's anthropology is thoroughly corporate, which goes against the grain of popular individualism in both church and society. Like Genesis 1–3, which speaks of the human race as one individual, *Adam*, Barth regularly portrays the one personal God in relationship to *der Mensch* ('man'), conceived as one corporate person. Questions concerning the activities of human individuals (*Menschen, Männer, Frauen*, men, human beings, men and women, etc.) are subordinate to this corporate anthropology. But this means that to try to make Barth's prose gender-neutral by employing the most popular (and stylistically most graceful) method – namely, by changing masculine singulars ('he') to gender-free plurals ('they') – would erase the corporate nature of Barth's anthropology and replace it with something quite foreign to his theological thinking – namely, speaking about humanity as though it were essentially a collection of individuals rather than a corporate entity standing before its Creator.

For all of these reasons, I have elected to leave the gendered language of Barth's text unchanged. This practice, I am convinced, is more honest and straightforward than the alternatives, and is meant not to preempt the important issues of theology and gender but to present a text in which they can be raised and debated.[2]

Although no footnotes appear in the original German, I have added two

kinds of notes to the translation. First, I have moved some of Barth's paren-
thetical references to the works he cites into endnotes in order to make the
main text more readable. Since few of these works are available in English,
the references are of limited usefulness to readers of the translation.
Second, I have added a few explanatory notes (indicated by a concluding
'*Trans.*'), most of which deal with terminology that would not otherwise be
clear to the English reader.

Barth's characteristic use of longer and shorter sections in small print
inserted periodically into his main text presents a challenge of a different
sort. Although not formally part of his dogmatics, they are too important to
be relegated to mere notes. Indeed, these fine-print passages contain some
of Barth's most important and fascinating asides, whether they contain
exegetical commentary, historical background, or arguments with other
theologians past and present. This new translation presents these excur-
suses in a typeface intended to make them more easily readable while still
indicating that they are subordinate to the main text.

I would like to acknowledge the many others who aided me in translating
this often difficult text into English – that is, if only I could remember
all of them! Gene Rogers translated the Latin passages that Barth cites
from various theologians of Protestant Orthodoxy, a task that exceeded
my linguistic skills. With regard to Barth's German, I have frequently
sought the help of colleagues in various places, including especially Joseph
Mangina and Geoffrey Atherton. George Hunsinger was of great help in
the vexing question of how to translate *Aufhebung*. I have also benefited
enormously from contributors to the German–English online translation
forum LEO ('Link Everything Online'),[3] a service of the Technische
Universität München, whom I know only by their screen names: especially
Peter <de>, Matthias <dt>, peter h. s., hm -- us, Anja, Jens, Werner, Hajo,
Gismo, willi, willi winzig, eastworld, hein mück, and Gerd – among others.
A special thanks is due to Paul Nimmo, who (at the instigation of Georgina
Brindley, my editor at T&T Clark) compared the entire translation to the
German original and not only saved me from some potentially embar-
rassing lapses but also suggested scores of improvements, most of which
I have adopted. Eugene Gallagher, with whom I designed and taught the
Theories of Religion seminar at Connecticut College, has supported this
project from the start. I would also like to acknowledge the financial support
of Connecticut College that enabled me to do part of the work in Germany,
and in particular to thank Frances Hoffmann, Dean of the Faculty. Finally,
I owe a word of both thanks and apology to Geoffrey Green, who originally accepted this project for T&T Clark (then in Edinburgh), then waited
patiently while I spent several years plodding through the job of translating
– but who eventually retired from the press before I managed to complete
the work.

Introduction: Barth as Theorist of Religion*

Garrett Green

Hans Frei, a Christian theologian teaching in a university department of religious studies, once made a passing comment about Karl Barth that says as much about contemporary intellectual culture as it does about Barth: 'Had he not been a theologian,' Frei remarked, 'he would have been more widely recognized as one of the towering minds of the twentieth century.'[1] Few who know his work would contest the fact that Barth (1886–1968) was the most influential Christian theologian of the past century – though many would hasten to distance themselves from his views. For Barth was nothing if not controversial, even contentious (one of his best-known works, bearing the terse title *Nein!*, is a ferocious attack on the views of his former colleague and countryman Emil Brunner). Though Barth was a Protestant – a native of German-speaking Switzerland who stood in the Reformed tradition stemming from Zwingli and Calvin in the sixteenth century – he has attracted a substantial following among Roman Catholics as well. As soon as one moves beyond the rarified company of clergy and professional theologians, however, Karl Barth's name recognition drops off precipitously.

Life and Work[2]

Born in Basel in 1886, Karl Barth came from a long line of Swiss Reformed clergymen and theologians on both sides of the family. He grew up in Berne, where his father was a professor in the theological faculty of the university, in a family devoted to books, music, and the outdoors. Like his father, Karl set out to become a theologian, studying first at his home university before moving on to sample the fruits of current German theology in Berlin,

---

* Portions of this introduction are adapted from my article 'Challenging the Religious Studies Canon: Karl Barth's Theory of Religion' in *The Journal of Religion*, 75 (October), 473–86.

1

Tübingen, and Marburg. His father, a theological conservative, tried to steer him away from Protestant Liberalism, the theological movement then in ascendancy. This attempt at paternal guidance, however, was no more successful than most such interventions, for in Berlin Karl heard lectures by the great liberal theologian Adolf von Harnack and eventually became the student of another leading liberal, Wilhelm Herrmann, in Marburg.

By the time he completed his studies in 1909, he had come to share the theology of his teachers, and he spent the following year working for a leading liberal journal, *Die Christliche Welt* ('The Christian World'). He next served for a year as assistant pastor at a church in Geneva where Calvin had once preached, before receiving a call in 1911 to a parish of his own in the small Swiss town of Safenwil. The decade he spent there in pastoral work changed his life and his theology. He became engaged and then married to Nelly Hoffmann, with whom he spent the rest of his life. As a pastor, he became embroiled in labour disputes involving his working-class congregation, while at the same time studying the writings of the burgeoning Religious Socialist movement and earning himself the nickname 'the Red pastor'. Like many young preachers before and since, he found that his theological education had not prepared him adequately for preaching and pastoral work, and he began to question the assumptions of the theological liberalism he had absorbed as a student. According to his later recollection, his final break with liberal theology was precipitated by an event shortly after German troops invaded neutral Belgium in 1914, igniting the First World War. When a manifesto supporting the Kaiser's war policy appeared over the signatures of ninety-three prominent German intellectuals, Barth was appalled to discover among them the names of his own revered teachers. 'In despair over what this indicated about the signs of the time,' he later wrote, 'I suddenly realized that I could not any longer follow either their ethics and dogmatics or their understanding of the Bible and of history. For me at least, 19th-century theology no longer held any future.'[3]

In the rethinking of theology that followed his break with Protestant Liberalism, Barth turned again to the Bible, which he now read with new eyes. Out of his intense studies over the next few years there emerged by 1919 a book – a commentary on Paul's letter to the Romans – that was destined to catapult him from obscure village parson to controversial theologian. The first edition of Barth's *Römerbrief*,[4] in the words of a contemporary Roman Catholic commentator, 'fell like a bombshell on the playground of the theologians'.[5] A second, thoroughly revised edition appeared in 1922, by which time Barth had already accepted a position as Honorary Professor of Reformed Theology at the University of Göttingen in Germany and his career as an academic theologian was launched. He moved on to a chair at the University of Münster in 1925, and five years later to the University of Bonn. There Barth wrote a small book on the medieval theologian Anselm of Canterbury, whom he credited with identifying the essential characteristic of the theologian's task in a phrase that served as the title of Barth's book: *Fides Quaerens Intellectum*, 'faith seeking understanding'. Rather than treating faith as something separated from another something called 'reason', to which it must then be related externally, Anselm speaks of the *fidei ratio*, the 'reason of faith' or 'faith's (own) reasoning'. Barth took from his study of Anselm the conviction that theology is by definition the *intellectus fidei*:[6] 'Theology is science seeking the knowledge of the Word of God spoken in God's work – science learning in the school of Holy Scripture ... [It is] the human logic of the divine Logos.'[7] Barth devoted the rest of his career to elaborating that Christian logic as he had come to understand it in volume after volume of the *Church Dogmatics*.

About the same time that he began work on his *magnum opus*, Barth found himself swept up into the political maelstrom that followed the ascension to power of the National Socialists and their *Führer*, Adolf Hitler, in 1933. An early leader in the resistance to attempts by the Nazi government to co-opt the Christian churches, and to their theological sympathizers known as the 'German Christians', Barth became the chief author of the Barmen Declaration, now widely acknowledged as one of the major confessional documents of modern Christianity. The church leaders and theologians who gathered in the industrial city of Barmen in May 1934 expressed in this brief text the theological basis for Christian opposition to Naziism and founded what came to be known as the Confessing Church. Barth himself soon came into conflict with the new German political leadership. Even before Barmen his refusal to begin every lecture with the 'Hitler salute', as required of all university professors, brought him under political scrutiny. When he subsequently refused to sign the oath of allegiance to Hitler required of all civil servants (including professors) – unless he could add the stipulation 'that I could be loyal to the Führer only within my responsibilities as an Evangelical Christian'[8] – he was barred from his classroom and charges were brought against him that led finally to his dismissal from his academic post in June 1935. He returned to Switzerland, where it took just two days for the University of Basel to appoint him to a chair in theology, which he held till the end of his career.

He spent the war years working on the *Church Dogmatics* while keeping in touch with friends and former colleagues in Germany. After the war he was invited back twice to lecture in Bonn; he played an active role in the burgeoning ecumenical movement; and he continued as always to comment on political developments as the Cold War got under way. Especially controversial was his steadfast refusal to equate Soviet communism with fascism while also opposing the rearmament of West Germany and maintaining contact with Christians in the communist nations of Eastern Europe. He continued working on the *Church Dogmatics* even beyond his retirement from teaching in 1962, but he eventually decided to leave the project unfinished (after publishing four of the projected five 'volumes', which actually comprised a total of thirteen part-volumes containing over 10,000 pages). He made his only trip to the United States following his retirement, giving lectures that were later published as part of *Evangelical Theology: An Introduction*. His ecumenical influence continued to grow, and he was especially surprised and encouraged by the warm reception of his theology by Roman Catholics; but he had to decline an invitation to be an official observer at the Second Vatican Council because of failing health.

Since Barth's death in 1968, interest in his thought has continued to grow as new generations have discovered the scope and power of his theological vision. There are also encouraging signs that the caricature of his theology that has inhibited an accurate assessment of his stature and significance may at last be giving way, especially in the work of younger scholars. It remains to be seen whether the field of religious studies will finally take note of a figure whose views on religion are among the most fascinating and original of the twentieth century.

Barth and Religious Studies

The neglect of Barth's thought by the intellectual elite of late Western modernity is reflected also in the absence of attention it receives from scholars of religion. We might have expected that the field of religious studies, at least, would pay closer attention to a figure who has played such a transformative role in a major world religion. The reasons for this neglect are various, but some of the main ones deserve to be mentioned.

First, Barth's published output is enormous, and he makes few concessions to those who might wish to catch the gist of his message in an article or two, or perhaps a short book. Although he did not begin his *magnum opus*, the *Church Dogmatics*, until mid-career, it had reached thirteen thick volumes by the time he broke off work on it, unfinished, late in life. And though it is surely his major achievement, it is far from being his only important writing. The book that launched his career as a public theologian, his commentary on Paul's Letter to the Romans (first published in 1919) will be discussed in some detail below. Throughout his life he kept up a breathtaking pace of teaching, public lectures, occasional writings, and preaching, and still found time to conduct a voluminous correspondence, much of which is now available in English. (Barth's life ended literally in mid-sentence: he had been working on a lecture he was scheduled to deliver, and set the manuscript aside before retiring; he died in his sleep during the night.)[9]

A second, and far more important, reason for his neglect by scholars of religion is the reputation – 'caricature' would be a more accurate term – that has dogged him since his earliest writings, a reputation that has been especially distorted in the English-speaking world. One index of the caricature is the apparently descriptive but in fact tendentious term 'neoorthodox' that is almost invariably attached to his name by commentators who are unsympathetic with, or ignorant of, his thought (the two are by no means incompatible). The term implies that his break with liberal theology was essentially reactionary, an attempt to return to an earlier stage in the history of doctrine. In fact, Barth's writing could more plausibly be labelled revolutionary, for he led theology in surprising new directions, in the course of which he sometimes broke dramatically with the orthodoxy even of his own Reformed tradition. The most striking examples are his doctrine of election and his theology of baptism. In the first case, he transforms Calvin's doctrine of 'double predestination' by focusing both damnation and salvation squarely on Jesus Christ, understanding him to be both the rejected one and the elected one – that is, the one elected to die on our behalf and thus to be rejected. In so doing Barth replaces the traditional Calvinist conception of a God who, by means of a hidden and inscrutable 'divine decree', condemns part of the human race to eternal damnation, with a God who freely takes upon himself the burden of our rejection, thereby freeing us from the consequences of our own sin. The other dramatic break with traditional Reformed teaching came at the very end of Barth's career, when he published one last fragment of the unfinished *Church Dogmatics* under the title *The Christian Life*. In the course of describing baptism as the foundation of that life, Barth rejects the practice of infant baptism, which both Luther and Calvin had retained. Though his theological reasoning is quite different from that of Baptists and Anabaptists, the little volume nevertheless provoked outrage among Barth's Reformed co-religionists. These radical revisions of tradition, however, have remained largely invisible behind the stubborn persistence of the caricature of Barth the intransigent 'neoorthodox' reactionary. Far more accurate is Robert Jenson's characterization of Barth as 'a theological questioner, a religious outsider, and a political left-winger'.[10]

A third reason for the neglect of Barth by scholars of religion brings us to the text presented here, which comprises the whole of §17 of the *Church Dogmatics* and contains Barth's theological interpretation of religion. In the original German, it bears the title 'Gottes Offenbarung als Aufhebung der Religion', which the English translators of the *Church Dogmatics* rendered 'The Revelation of God as the Abolition of Religion'. The problem is that 'abolition' is a grossly inadequate and wholly misleading translation of *Aufhebung*, the term that is the key to the logic of Barth's theological theory of religion. Though it would be difficult to prove, I am convinced that this single prominent mistranslation has played a crucial role in encouraging the caricature of Barth's theology that has for so long distorted its reception in the English-speaking world. To be sure, one can sympathize with the translators, faced with the perplexing career of the verb *aufheben* in German philosophy since Hegel. J. Glenn Gray's explanation of the term covers the essential points:

The German verb *aufheben* means literally 'to lift something up' – e.g. an apple from the ground. But figuratively and intellectually it has two other, seemingly contradictory connotations. For one thing, it means 'to preserve or save or store up'; for another, it means 'to cancel out or annul'. This double meaning of a single, ordinary German word Hegel seizes upon as the core of his dialectical method of interpreting the past, a method which has played a momentous role down to the present. The historical past of individuals, peoples, even epochs is, according to him, a continuous process of cancelling out or annulling that past and yet at the same time preserving its essentials in a higher synthesis, which is a blend of the old and the new, the past and the present.[11]

Barth – who, like other German-speaking intellectuals in the nineteenth and twentieth centuries, imbibed the language of German Idealism with his mother's milk – has borrowed this favourite Hegelian term and put it to his own use. As in Hegel, so in Barth, *Aufhebung* is a key to the *logic* of the argument, a logic that can be appropriately termed dialectical for both, though in quite different senses. Barth, committed as he is to a concretely theological method, cannot accept Hegel's interpretation of religion and Christianity in terms of a dialectical philosophy of history. But he shares with Hegel the conviction that the truth can only be told by saying both no and yes; and he finds in the unique ambiguity of the verb *aufheben* a way of articulating their dialectical interrelationship.

It is my hope that the availability of a fresh and accurate English translation of Barth's major treatment of the concept of religion will encourage scholars and students of religion to undertake a serious and thoughtful engagement with his ideas. I want to begin the process by presenting Karl Barth's theory of religion in the same way that any theory should be presented in religious studies: by describing its presuppositions, methodology, and leading concepts before subjecting it to critical evaluation and comparison with other positions.

Religion in the Early Barth

Although the concept of religion played a significant role in Barth's earliest period – while he was a pastor in Safenwil and before his commentary on Romans catapulted him into notoriety – its prominence as an organizing category emerged only in the revised edition of the *Römerbrief* in 1922. Typical of his early treatment of religion is its role in a now-famous lecture he delivered in 1916, the year he began work on the *Romans* commentary, entitled 'The Strange New World within the Bible'.[12] It presents in clear and forceful terms the theology of the young Barth who had broken decisively with his liberal teachers. 'It is not the right human thoughts about God which form the content of the Bible,' he says (explicitly rejecting a key liberal premise), 'but the right divine thoughts about men. The Bible tells us not how we should talk with God but what he says to us ...' (43). The heart of the lecture is constructed around three answers to the question 'What is there within the Bible?': history, morality, and religion. The context makes clear that he chooses the concept of religion because, like the concepts of history and morality, it plays a key role in theological liberalism. The three answers are those typically given by the regnant liberal theology of the day. Religion, on this account, is 'defined as what we are to think concerning God, how we are to find him, and how we are to conduct ourselves in his presence' (41). In a manner that remained typical of Barth's thinking to the end of his life, he does not simply reject this definition; he does not deny but rather affirms that the Bible contains history, morality, and religion. The Bible really *is* 'a treasury of truth concerning the right relation of men to the eternal and divine', but it also contains something far more important, 'something greater' than religion (41). He affirms that the older orthodoxy was right in its insistence that 'there is revelation in the Bible and not religion only' (44). But he can also, even in this earliest period, occasionally use 'religion' to describe the Bible's more-than-human content: 'in the Bible ... the theme is, so to speak, the religion of God and never once the religion of the Jews, or Christians, or heathen ...' (45). This passage illustrates another characteristic feature of Barth's theology of religion that he never abandoned: his relativizing of Christianity by placing it within the series of human religions.

Barth could hardly be described as having a *theory* of religion before 1922, since the topic, strictly speaking, was not of his own choosing. He comes to speak of religion because of the important role it plays in the thought of his theological opponents. Adolf von Harnack and other theologians of Protestant liberalism, not Barth, are the ones who made of 'religion' a central theme of Christian theology.[13] In the course of arguing that they are wrong, Barth finds himself drawn into the modern discussion of religion.

The Romans Commentary: Religion as an Organizing Concept

The treatment of religion in the first edition of Barth's *Römerbrief* is essentially the one epitomized in the 1916 lecture. References to religion appear frequently in the text, typically in parallel with morality ('*Religion und Moral*' is a constantly recurring phrase), and nearly always in negative contrast to the gospel. No sooner had the book achieved notice than its author was hard at work on a revision, completed in 1921 and published the following year. As he noted himself, in the second edition 'hardly one stone remains upon another' from the original version.[14]

One of the stones displaced in the reconstruction of the *Römerbrief* was the concept of religion. What had been a favourite but nontechnical term in the first edition becomes a structural element in the radically revised second edition. The shift is already evident in the table of contents. In both editions the commentary is organized into chapters exactly corresponding to the chapters in Paul's epistle, to which Barth gives brief thematic titles. Each chapter is further subdivided into two to four sections (each covering a specified portion of Paul's text), to which Barth likewise assigns titles. In view of the thoroughgoing revision of the book, this overall organization remains surprisingly similar in the 1922 version. Especially illuminating for our topic is the seventh chapter, which bears the title 'Freedom' in both editions. References to religion were densely concentrated here in the 1919 edition, when Barth had chosen his subtitles from Paul's own categories. In the revised edition, however, religion emerges for the first time as an organizing concept in new section headings:

		1919 Edition	1922 Edition
Rom. 7:1–6		The New Being	The Limit of Religion
Rom. 7:7–13		The Law and Romanticism	The Meaning of Religion
Rom. 7:14–25		The Law and Pietism	The Reality of Religion

These titles make evident what has happened: the Pauline term 'law' has been replaced by the modern term 'religion'. Barth assumes that the way to make Paul's talk of the law speak to twentieth-century readers is to talk about religion. As the details of his commentary on Romans 7 demonstrate, he takes religion to be the functional equivalent for modern people of the Jewish law for Paul's contemporaries. 'Religion', Barth comments on Rom. 7:11, 'is that human necessity in which the power exercised over men by sin is clearly demonstrated.'[15]

The second edition of the *Römerbrief* bears the marks of Barth's recent exposure to existentialist ideas, especially through his reading of Kierkegaard and Dostoevsky, both of whom he cites repeatedly in chapter 7. The influence of existentialism on his theory of religion is evident from the title of the opening section: he now conceives of religion as the limit or frontier (*die Grenze*) of human existence, where we encounter 'an inexorable and predetermined "either-or"'. Here we confront the 'final and impossible possibility' of human life, 'the last human possibility – the possibility of Religion' (229). It is not simply that religion exposes the limited quality of human existence; rather, religion *is* that limit, it is defined as such. 'The limit of religion and the unavoidable problematic into which precisely it plunges man, is thus identical with the limit of the humanly possible in general.'[16] The controlling metaphor is of a realm (the human) whose outer boundary (religion) is at once its limit and its point of contact with that which lies beyond it (the divine). Like the theologians of the nineteenth century before him, Barth identifies the essentially human with the essentially religious. But unlike those theologians, he characterizes it in dialectical, even contradictory, terms. He seizes upon this theme in Dostoevsky and Kierkegaard to bash complacent modern liberals over the head. Nothing more enraged the early Barth than pietistic or romantic accounts of religion as the realm of comfort or peace:

> Religion is anything but harmony with oneself, much less with the infinite. There is no room here for lofty feelings or noble humanity. Let naive central and west Europeans think so for as long as they can. Here is the abyss; here is terror. Here one sees demons (Ivan Karamazov *and* Luther!).[17]

Reduced to a formula: 'The meaning of religion is death' (Barth's epitome of the third subsection, 'The Meaning of Religion'). In accordance with the parallel between religion and the law, he is careful, despite the negativity of his account of religion, not to deny its essential place or simply to identify it with sin:

> Religion is no more [to be identified with] sin than is any other human possibility, because sin is much more than *a* possibility. On the contrary: religion marks the point where all human possibilities enter the light of the divine. It represents the divine, it is its delegation, its offprint, its negative – outside of the divine itself.[18]

Religion, then, is negative in the same way as a photographic negative: it shows reality as it is, but in negative rather than positive images. Nowhere is the existentialism of the early Barth more evident than in the close association of religion with death:

> For religion *is* the *adversary*, the *adversary* of man, of the Greek and the barbarian, disguised as the truest friend; it is the *krisis* of civilization and uncivilization. It is the *most dangerous* adversary that man has this side of death (apart from God). For it is the human possibility of recalling that we must die, the possibility of recalling God.[19]

Although Barth will later reject the kind of existential anthropology presented here so melodramatically, nothing he says about religion is incompatible with his later views.

How Barth Changed His Mind

Yet something important does change between the 1922 *Romans* commentary and Barth's mature theology, which he presented in a series of volumes of the *Church Dogmatics*, beginning in 1932 and continuing into the 1960s. Though it would be difficult to find a specific assertion about religion in the earlier book that he would repudiate later, there is nevertheless a significant shift in Barth's theory of religion. The most visible sign of the change in Barth's thinking was his abandonment of the projected multivolume *Christian Dogmatics* after the publication of the first instalment in 1927.[20] When the editors of the *Christian Century* asked Barth in 1938 to summarize for American readers the changes that his theology had undergone in the previous decade, he responded with this self-interpretation:

> ... in these years I have had to rid myself of the last remnants of a philosophical, i.e., anthropological (in America one says 'humanistic' or 'naturalistic') foundation and exposition of Christian doctrine.[21]

He calls 'the real document of this farewell' his small book on Anselm's argument for God[22] rather than his notorious *Nein!* to Emil Brunner in 1934.[23] His new methodological commitment he now calls 'a christological concentration',[24] and we will examine its consequences for the way in which he understands religion in the *Church Dogmatics*. In a 1956 essay on 'The Humanity of God' Barth is even willing to call the one-sidedness of his early theology heretical, though he continues to maintain that his position had been correct as far as it had gone.[25] In its exclusive emphasis on the 'wholly other' God of the Bible, he admits, dialectical theology treated the deity of God 'in isolation, abstracted and absolutized, and set it over against man, this miserable wretch'.[26] This theology, justifiable as it was in response to the humanistic excesses of liberal theology, failed to employ the 'christological concentration', the necessity of viewing every Christian teaching from the perspective of Jesus Christ, and therefore overlooked the fact that 'it is precisely God's *deity* which, rightly understood, includes his *humanity*'.[27] It is not simply that Barth's early theology grasped one aspect, God's divinity, while missing an additional item, his humanity; rather, the divinity itself was inadequately understood because it was conceived 'abstractly', that is, apart from the concrete reality of Jesus Christ. 'Thus,' Barth summarizes, 'we have here no universal deity capable of being reached conceptually, but this concrete deity – real and recognizable in the *descent* grounded in that sequence and peculiar to the existence of Jesus Christ.'[28]

Not only the doctrine of God but every Christian doctrine appears in a new light when approached according to Barth's new-found methodological clarity – by a method that is concretely *christological* and therefore *narrative* rather than abstractly philosophical. The concept of religion, too, undergoes this transformation, and we need to look at it afresh in the context of Barth's thought after his turning-point, which means in the grand theological context of the *Church Dogmatics*.

Revelation as the Sublimation of Religion

Context is an important key to Barth's theory of religion. As significant as any particular statement he makes about religion is the place it occupies in his mature theological enterprise. In his own terms, proper context makes the difference between 'abstract' thinking about God in general and 'concrete' theological understanding of God in his historical revelation in Jesus Christ. The concept of religion, originally important to Barth because of its role in the programme of liberal theology, eventually finds its place in the *theological* context of the *Church Dogmatics*. When Barth began publishing part-volumes of his *magnum opus* in the early 1930s, he made a conscious and explicit break in method from the practice of Protestant theologians since Schleiermacher. Like the theologians of the previous century, Barth begins the project of dogmatics by addressing the questions of how theology is possible and what method is appropriate to the undertaking. Unlike his modern forebears, however, he does not treat these matters as 'prolegomena', that is, they do not constitute an essentially nontheological introduction to, and justification of, theology in terms of some allegedly general or universal human knowledge.[29] Rather, for Barth, questions of definition and method are themselves theological; they do not precede dogmatics proper but are a constitutive part thereof. Thus volume one of the *Church Dogmatics*, published in two parts in 1932, is not entitled 'Introduction' or 'Prolegomena' but *The Doctrine of the Word of God*. Theology, he insists, can only be theologically defined.

This theological introduction to theology in the first volume of the *Church Dogmatics* is the context for Barth's most developed treatment of religion, presented here in a fresh and more accurate translation.[30] This context makes clear that Barth's theory of religion can only be a theology of religion; any other approach would be 'abstract' and thus inappropriate to theology. Barth follows German academic tradition by stating a thesis at the outset of each section, which he proceeds to develop and defend in the subsequent discussion. The thesis statement of this section (§17) contains Barth's formal theological definition of religion:

> God's revelation in the outpouring of the Holy Spirit is the judging, but also reconciling, presence of God in the world of human religion – that is, in the realm of attempts by man to justify and sanctify himself before a willfully and arbitrarily devised image of God. The church is the site of true religion to the extent that through grace it lives by grace. (1)

Barth means two things by saying that revelation is the sublimation of religion: (1) that Christians, on the basis of God's self-revelation in Jesus Christ must say a resounding *no* to human religion; and (2) that on the same basis they may also say a qualified *yes* to religion. The first point is

11

a familiar theme from Barth's earlier writings, especially *Romans*; in this sense *Aufhebung* does indeed mean 'abolition'. The second point, though implicit in the early Barth, now emerges with new clarity on the basis of the 'christological concentration'. It allows the 'later' Barth to say, in words that one can scarcely imagine on the lips of the 'early' Barth, that *'the Christian religion is the true religion'* (85; Barth's emphasis).[31] The dialectical logic encapsulated in the concept of sublimation is evident in the structure of Barth's presentation: in a way foreshadowed a decade earlier in the tripartite subdivision of the discussion of religion in the *Römerbrief*, he structures his theology of religion in terms of what we might call three dialectical 'moments':

1. The Problem of Religion in Theology
2. Religion as Faithlessness
3. The True Religion

As in any dialectical argument, the challenge of interpreting Barth on religion is to strike just the right balance between the opposing vectors of thesis and antithesis. The price of taking statements out of context is even higher than in the case of other kinds of texts: it can lead to such commonly heard errors as that Barth advocates the 'abolition of religion', or that he denies that Christianity is a religion.[32]

Religion as a Theological Problem

Nothing so marks the *Church Dogmatics* as a work of *modern* theology as its explicit attention to religion. Early in our text Barth surveys the history of the concept of religion (37–45) in a lengthy excursus (one of those passages in small print sprinkled liberally throughout the *Church Dogmatics* containing Barth's historical, exegetical, and polemical asides). Beginning with Thomas Aquinas and Calvin but concentrating on the Lutheran and Reformed Orthodox theologians of the seventeenth and eighteenth centuries, Barth tells the 'sad story' (*Trauergeschichte*, 44) of the gradual emergence of religion as 'an independent known quantity alongside revelation' until at last *'religion is not to be understood from the point of view of revelation, but rather revelation from that of religion'* (45; Barth's emphasis). This modern Christian heresy, which he dubs 'religionism', poses the problem to which part one of our text is devoted: its ascendancy means that theology was 'no longer taking itself seriously as theology' (45). Barth sets himself the task of correcting the course of theology by restoring religion to its proper place.

The first step, establishing the proper context, takes place in the opening paragraph, which amounts to a capsule summary of Barth's theological method. 'The event of God's revelation', he begins, 'is to be understood and presented here as it is attested to the church of Jesus Christ by the Holy Scripture' (33). The little qualifier 'here' (omitted in the original translation) is a subtle signal of Barth's 'postmodern'[33] sensibility: it acknowledges implicitly that there may well be other ways to approach religion and revelation while nevertheless insisting on the necessity of *this* approach if one is to do theology rather than something else. Echoing the theme of his bitter debate with Emil Brunner in 1934, Barth explicitly rejects any human 'point of contact' (*Anknüpfungspunkt*) for revelation. In a characteristic move, he reverses the familiar logical pattern, insisting that 'both the *actuality* and the *possibility*' of the revelatory event are grounded in God. Against virtually the entire modern theological establishment, Barth refuses on principle to provide a philosophical or anthropological foundation for theology.[34] Revelation is 'a self-enclosed circle', lending to theology, as he elsewhere comments, the character of a 'virtuous circle'.[35] Because this self-enclosed event encounters us in the real world of human culture, however, we are unavoidably confronted with the problem of religion. Virtually alone among modern interpreters of religion, Barth does not begin with the empirical fact of religion, either objectively or subjectively, individually or communally. Rather, he begins 'from above' with divine revelation, whose narrative logic then leads to a consideration of religion. Barth thus belongs among those theorists of religion who approach the subject indirectly, out of a primary interest in some other issue. A parallel might be found in a thinker like Freud, who likewise comes to religion out of a prior interest in something else: he finds that he must deal with religion because of the psychological power of human wishes. Thus just as Barth, guided by his theological interest, defines religion in terms of divine revelation, so Freud, guided by his psychoanalytic interest, defines religion in terms of human desires.[36]

After establishing the theological context and corresponding methodology, Barth turns to the issue of religion. Because revelation, the subject matter of theology, 'also has at least the character and face of a human, historically and psychologically comprehensible, phenomenon into whose nature, structure, and value one may inquire as in the case of other human phenomena' (34), we are led unavoidably to the problem of human religion. Here Barth stands with the secular theorists of his day, emphasizing that religion, including quite explicitly the Christian religion, is to be studied historically and comparatively. 'Viewed from this aspect,' he insists, 'what we call revelation necessarily appears as something particular in the field of the universal that one calls religion – as "Christianity" or "Christian religion" – one predicate of a subject that can have other predicates as well, one species in a genus to which other species belong as well' (34). As such, Christianity is surely 'peculiar' (*eigenartig*) but not 'unique' (*einzigartig*),[37] 'remarkable' (*erstaunlich*) but not 'incomprehensible' (*unbegreiflich*). Not only does Barth permit the relativizing of Christianity among the religions of the world but he positively insists upon it – and on theological grounds: 'We would be denying revelation as such if we should wish to dispute the fact that it is also' human religion.[38] It could be argued that the relationship of theology and religious studies in contemporary North American academia is better suited to Barth's understanding of their relationship than was his own European context, in which theology was (and still is) largely isolated from non-theological religious studies.

Having made clear that revelation appears as religion, Barth turns to his main point, the theological problem posed by this fact. Briefly stated, because revelation assumes the historical and social form of religion, theologians run the risk of misconstruing the *relationship* of revelation and religion, a risk to which they have in fact succumbed by reversing the proper priority. The problem – he calls it a 'catastrophe' (42) – first appeared at the start of the eighteenth century in the movement called rational orthodoxy. The outcome was 'Neoprotestantism', Barth's term for the predominant direction of theology over the past three centuries, whose definitive characteristic is precisely 'religionism': the 'reversal of revelation and religion' that has produced such disastrous results for theology (47). The problem is not that modern theology has attributed a religious character to revelation but rather that it has made religion into the criterion of revelation rather than the other way around. Despite the self-understanding of Neoprotestant theologians as defenders of free inquiry, Barth attributes their thinking to uncertainty, and ultimately to lack of faith. They 'fell prey to the absolutism by which the man of that age made himself the center, measure, and end of all things' (48).[39]

The theological task at hand is therefore to establish the priority of revelation over religion without denying the religious nature of revelation. A simple inversion of the Neoprotestant error, however, is not the answer. One could say (though Barth does not put it in these terms) that 'revelationism' is no antidote to 'religionism'. The error of both is that they treat revelation and religion as coordinate realities susceptible to conceptual control. 'It always indicates a crucial misunderstanding,' Barth declares categorically, 'if one even tries to classify revelation and religion systematically, that is, to juxtapose them as comparable spheres, to mark them off from each other, and to set them in relationship to one another' (49). Here the dialectical emphasis of *Romans* remains unmitigated, still expressed with a hint of Kierkegaard: the relation of revelation and religion is a matter of 'either–or' – something that the scientific advocates of *Religionswissenschaft* understand better than the theologians (50). Barth's insistence on discontinuity leads him so far as to claim that 'revelation is denied whenever it is treated as problematic' (51).[40] The problem of religion is vital because it is just one aspect of a broader issue. The logic of either–or is unavoidable because revelation means beginning with the lordship of Jesus Christ, the sovereignty of God over all human affairs, including religion. The methodological problem raised by religion is thus a microcosm of theological method generally.

Only at the end of the treatment of 'The Problem of Religion in Theology' (the title of part one) does the 'later' Barth – who abandoned his first dogmatics after reading Anselm – come clearly into focus. Only after rejecting not just Neoprotestant 'religionism' but any '*systematic* coordination of God and man, of revelation and religion', does he offer a positive alternative: Barth's alternative to Neoprotestant 'religionism' is 'telling the *story* [*Geschichte*] that is enacted' between God and man, revelation and religion (51).[41] Proceeding narratively rather than systematically by applying the 'christological concentration', theology discovers the appropriate analogy for relating religion and revelation in the incarnation of Christ. The dialectic of discontinuity is thereby complemented by the 'analogy of faith', and the result brings us back to the pivotal term *Aufhebung* in the concluding sentence of the first part: 'Remembering the christological doctrine of the incarnation, and applying it logically, we speak of revelation as the sublimation of religion' (52).[42]

Religion as Faithlessness

The first of the three parts comprising Barth's treatment of religion has set the stage for the dialectic of religion and revelation by positing the thesis that revelation necessarily assumes a religious form in the human world, and that Christianity is therefore a religion. Part two now calls it radically into question by developing the antithesis: that religion is the faithless attempt to deny God's self-revelation. This clash will prepare the way for the third and final part, in which the opposition between thesis and antithesis will be 'sublimated' (*aufgehoben*), enabling theology to speak of Christianity as the true religion. The contrast is apparent in their titles: 'Religion as Faithlessness' is followed by 'The True Religion'. How, the reader may ask, is the latter topic possible if the former is true? It would appear to involve some such absurdity as 'true faithlessness'. Or perhaps the former title is mere hyperbole and the author really means to speak only of the *apparent* faithlessness of religion. But Barth, we soon learn, means precisely what he says: both the thesis and the antithesis are to be affirmed – according to the logic of christological sublimation. (The point could be stated epigrammatically: theology is 'Christo-logical'.) In order to see how Barth is able to affirm both of these apparently contradictory propositions, we will need to examine in some detail how the dialectical logic of sublimation actually works.

Before launching his theological assault on religion, Barth inserts a caveat, a kind of plea for mercy on behalf of religion, which should be treated, he says, with the 'patience of Christ'. He warns specifically against the favourite apologetic ploy of modern theologians: using a concept of the 'essence' (*Wesen*) of religion to argue that Christianity is the highest religion.[43] But he is equally critical of modern Enlightenment 'toleration', which he characterizes as the arrogance of the *aufklärerischer Besserwisser*, the know-it-all condescension of rationalist thinkers who place themselves above the religious fray. He devotes an excursus to Lessing as the prototype of this stance and assigns Hegel's philosophy of religion to the same category. This kind of tolerance, he argues, 'is in fact the worst kind of intolerance'. Conversely, the christological exclusivism that Barth advocates, typically assumed to be intolerant, in fact offers the only basis for a genuine tolerance, namely, the 'patience of Christ' (54–5).

Barth introduces the negative thesis of the dialectic of religion, familiar from his earlier writings, with characteristic bluntness: 'religion is *faith-lessness*; religion is a concern – one must say, in fact, *the* concern – of *godless* man' (55). He backs up this thesis with a citation from Luther that includes the charge that 'the piety of man is sheer blasphemy of God and the greatest sin a man commits', thus showing that theological critique of religion is hardly original with Barth; indeed, it is a common theme in the Protestant Reformers. Barth will not even agree that the thesis is negative: on the basis of the preceding argument, he insists, 'this proposition ... can have nothing to do with a negative value judgment' (55). This seemingly incredible claim is Barth's dramatic way of reminding his readers that the entire line of argument is strictly *theological*. The identification of religion with unbelief is not advanced as a conclusion of comparative religion, or as a judgment of philosophy of religion based on some notion of the essence of religion. More important, it is directed not just against other religions but against Christian religion as well. 'Precisely because it is intended only to express the judgment of God', he writes, 'it signifies no human disparagement of human values, no dispute about the true, the good, and the beautiful, which upon closer examination we can discover in nearly all religions, and which we naturally expect to find in particularly abundant measure in our own religion, if we hold to it with any conviction' (56). In an excursus inserted at this point, Barth specifically warns against the sort of Christian iconoclasm that has sometimes been justified by appeal to the divine judgment against human religion. Religion stands under *God's* judgment in precisely the same way that everything human does; it is a misuse of this truth to turn it into a *human* judgment against religion in particular. On the contrary, Barth affirms, 'In the sphere of reverence before God, the reverence before human greatness must always have its place; it is subject to God's judgment, not ours' (56). This aspect of Barth's theory of religion is especially important for religious studies, since it clearly precludes the frequent tendency to dismiss Barth as a detractor of religion or as a Christian imperialist passing lofty judgments against other religions.

To say in English, as the translation in the *Church Dogmatics* does, that for Barth religion is 'unbelief' risks misunderstanding the point he is making. German uses the word *Glaube* to indicate what is covered in English by both 'belief' and 'faith'. In characterizing religion as *Unglaube*, Barth has in mind not primarily 'beliefs' or doctrines but rather a lack of *faith*, in the Reformation sense of *fiducia*, trust or confidence in the promises of God. Religion, Barth is saying, is an expression of faithlessness, the proclivity of human beings to disbelieve God's assurance of salvation in Christ and to rely instead on their own resources.

He develops the thesis in two constructive propositions. First, revelation is God's offering and presentation of himself (57). The ability to know God is therefore based solely on God's self-revelation, not on an inherent human religious capacity. Moreover, that capacity, far from aiding in the knowledge of God, shows itself to be resistance to God's revelation. Citing Calvin's assertion that the human spirit is a veritable factory of idols, Barth argues that the characteristically religious activity is the setting up of man-made idols in place of God, and that revelation consequently cannot attach itself to them but must first remove them. He secures the point biblically in an excursus on the theme of idolatry in the Old and New Testaments (59–64). Second, Barth maintains, revelation is the act by which God through grace reconciles humanity to himself. Again, the point is to show the incompatibility between human religion and divine revelation. Since the practical aim of all human religious activity is self-justification and self-sanctification, it constitutes a barrier that must first be removed before people can receive revelation, which comes only by grace. Barth secures this proposition, too, exegetically in an excursus on law and gospel in scripture (67–72).

Barth is also convinced that we can observe on an 'immanent' level a corresponding 'inner dialectic' that confirms the fact that religion, even on its own terms, is ultimately self-contradictory and impossible. This discussion lends itself particularly well to religious studies, since Barth in effect temporarily lays aside the mantle of theologian and tries his hand at a kind of phenomenological analysis of religion and culture. Religion, he tries to show, betrays its ultimate *non-necessity* by assuming that the need for God can be fulfilled. Religion – Barth even calls it 'the actual religious essence of man' (73) – is precisely the externalization of that need. Here Barth comes close to Ludwig Feuerbach's theory of religion (which he always took seriously) as the objectification of human ideals, as well as to Freud's psychological adaptation of projection theory. Along with its non-necessity, religion also betrays a fundamental *weakness* that becomes evident with historical change. Whenever human culture changes, Barth observes, religion is faced with a dilemma: either it will deny its ultimacy by changing itself, or else by refusing to change it will become obsolete.

The upshot of this 'immanent' dialectic is that religion always tends towards a critical turning point, a crisis that occurs whenever the attempted religious projection fails, driving human beings in one of two directions: mysticism or atheism. The conservative form of religious crisis, mysticism (he calls it 'esoteric atheism', 80), does not attack religion directly but undermines it by rejecting all its external forms in favour of their inner, 'spiritual' meaning. Nevertheless, Barth astutely observes, mystics love the externals of religion because they need them as material for their spiritualizing reinterpretation. Atheism, on the other hand, lives by sheer negation and therefore, unlike mysticism, overlooks the fact that negation makes sense only against the background of a relative affirmation. By concentrating exclusively on the denial of God and his law, the atheist, again unlike the mystic, overlooks other potentially religious dogmas and certainties. But atheism, Barth concludes, is the stronger of the two forms, which share the common programme of negating the transcendent world of religion – a programme which cannot succeed in the end, since sheer negation is not only sterile but clears the way for new divinities – and with them new religious movements – to arise.

Barth's brief excursion into phenomenology of religion shows him to be in general agreement with the dominant tendency in sociology of religion since Durkheim that interprets religion as a structural aspect of human societies. Like most sociological theory, but unlike the philosophy of religion of his day, Barth treats religion not as a universal essence but as an ongoing and ever-changing dialectic of forces within human communities. He credits religion with enormous social power, while at the same time evaluating it as negatively as any secular sociologist – indeed, more negatively than most. Religion, for Barth the phenomenologist, is both inevitable and futile, leading to a sterile cycle of religious affirmation, crisis, and breakdown, followed by the outbreak of new religious movements condemned to repeat the process. Religions die, Barth claims, not as a result of the principled attack of mysticism or atheism but rather because they are defeated by other religions (82).

The 'real crisis of religion', Barth maintains, returning to his properly theological argument, cannot originate from within the 'magic circle of religion' but must break in from beyond, which means from beyond the human realm altogether (83). The theological point of his phenomenological assessment is thus to show how much greater is the challenge to religion that comes from revelation than from any conceivable historical or ideological attack upon it. Once again the crucial concept appears at the turning point of the argument: 'That sublimation of religion, however, which signifies a real and dangerous assault upon it', he writes in the final sentence of part two, 'is found in another book, in comparison to which the books of mysticism and atheism can only be described as utterly harmless' (84).

18

Christianity as the True Religion

After so powerful an exposition of the thesis that religion is *Unglaube*, lack of faith, it is difficult to imagine how for Barth religion could have any positive significance. The double meaning of *Aufhebung* ('sublimation') in the title, however, is a clue that there is more to the story of religion. Recall that Barth warned at the outset against the temptation to deny the religious nature of revelation. Now in part three he sets out to make good on these claims. 'The sublimation of religion by revelation', he writes, 'does not only have to mean its negation, not only the judgment that religion is faithlessness' (85). Barth discovers the key to the theological dialectic of religion in an analogy. In the opening statement of the third part ('The True Religion'), Barth announces that 'we can talk about "true" religion only in the sense in which we talk about a "justified sinner"' (85).

This metaphor, which encapsulates the heart of the Reformation doctrine of justification by faith, controls Barth's subsequent discussion. So it is important to examine it closely as the key to his theory of religion. Faithless religion is related to true religion, Barth is saying, as the fallen sinner is related to the 'new man' in Christ. Using the christological dialectic Barth has developed, one could paraphrase the doctrine this way: justification is the sublimation of the sinner; the antithesis of human sin and divine justice is sublimated in the cross of Christ. The important point for the theory of religion is that the sinner does not cease to be a sinner when he is justified: he is righteous only in the dialectical reality of the 'justified sinner'. In other words, the thesis ('man is a sinner') does not cease to be true because of the antithesis ('man is justified'); both remain true in the relationship of sublimation. To use Hegelian language, justification is the 'negation of the negative', not a simple positive. One does not leave the previous reality behind but carries it along (as negated and overcome) into the new reality.

The implications for religion are straightforward, once the analogy has been grasped and properly applied. Barth puts it in general terms like this: 'No religion *is* true. A religion can only *become* true' (85). Just as in the case of the sinner, such a transformation can come only *'from without'*, only from a reality that is alien and incomprehensible from the sinner's own perspective. In a nutshell: 'Like the justified man, the true religion is a creature of *grace.'* Religion, without ceasing to be faithlessness in so far as it remains a product of human culture and imagination, can nevertheless *become* true – by the grace of God. But Barth takes one further logical step at this point, one grounded in the reversal of possibility and actuality so basic to his theological method. We know that it is possible for a religion to become true, not because of some abstract reasoning about what God can do, but only on the basis of the actuality. That is, we know that God can make a religion true because he has done so.

19

We have now reached the climax of Barth's entire argument, the linchpin of his theological theory of religion:

> There is a true religion: just as there is a justified sinner. As long as we remain strictly and precisely within this analogy – and it is more than an analogy, for in the broad sense it is the very matter that we are dealing with here – we must not hesitate to state that *the Christian religion is the true religion*. (85)

Hardly has Barth uttered this thesis than he is already warning against its possible misunderstanding and abuse. He is especially concerned to emphasize that it may not be interpreted 'as a polemic against the non-Christian religions that might have served as preparation for the proposition that the Christian religion is the true religion'. Eschewing all such self-interested contrasts between Christianity and the 'idolatry and works-righteousness' of other religions, Barth points out that such a line of argument would amount to denying that Christianity is a religion at all – a claim that would contradict the very theological truth that he is here affirming. Stated positively, the point is that the identification of Christianity as the true religion can only be understood as a faith statement. Barth is not proposing yet another variant of the favourite modern apologetic that portrays Christianity as the highest form of religion, the culmination of an historical or evolutionary process. All such apologetics are undialectical because they fail to apply divine judgment to Christianity. In Barth's theory the judgment against human religion falls on the Christian religion quite as much as on other forms. In what must surely count as the most extreme statement of his polemic against religion, Barth inserts a lengthy excursus at this point detailing 'the necessary struggle of revelation against the religion of revelation', which includes this italicized formula: '*The religion of revelation is indeed bound to God's revelation, but God's revelation is not bound to the religion of revelation*' (88–9). So worried is Barth that his thesis will be taken as justification for Christian triumphalism, that much of part three – intended to bring out the *positive* sense of the sublimation of religion – is in fact devoted to further securing the negative thesis (already the subject of part two) that religion – *all* religion – is faithlessness.

What is remarkable about Barth's argument is that he can nevertheless affirm, on the basis of divine revelation, that Christianity is the true religion. Seemingly aware that his emphasis on the negative threatens to undercut his positive thesis, Barth hastens to assure us that 'this relativizing of the Christian religion' does not imply that Christian faith is 'disheartened, insecure, or weak', or that the 'decision for the truth of the Christian religion might thereby be robbed of its power or confidence' (91). His point, rather, is that Christian power and confidence rest utterly on the grace of God and are in no way attributable to human achievement. So foreign is this way of thinking to modern theorists of religion (theologians included), that it requires great effort to hear what Barth is really saying. From the perspective of religious studies it should be abundantly clear that Barth is making no claim whatsoever for the superiority of Christianity on historical, philosophical, phenomenological, comparative – or any other non-theological – grounds. His argument does not imply that anyone ought to be persuaded that Christianity is the true religion for any reason other than that God's Holy Spirit moves him or her to faith. For those who claim to speak on the basis of such faith, however – and that rightfully includes all Christian theologians – the thesis that Christianity is the true religion is an inescapable consequence of their proper starting point, namely, God's self-revelation in Jesus Christ.

In considering the relationship of Christianity to the other religions, Barth rarely enters into their specific characteristics. This reticence makes sense on the basis of his strictly theological methodology. What business has the Christian theologian, whose task is the explication and elaboration of divine revelation in Jesus Christ, in commenting on the teachings and practices of other religions? To do so would appear to be, on the one hand, irrelevant and on the other, arrogant. It is therefore particularly noteworthy that Barth makes a rare exception in the case of Pure-Land Buddhism. The context of this digression is Barth's consideration of grace as the ground of Christian truth. Acknowledging 'the victorious *grace* of God as the mystery of the truth of the Christian religion' means that Christianity (especially in its Protestant expression) is pre-eminently 'the religion of free grace' (100). This conclusion raises the question of whether there might not be *other* religions of grace. If there are, it would seem, they cannot be irrelevant to theology; for their existence would undermine the claim that the Christian religion is *the* true religion. So at just this point Barth inserts a discussion of what he takes to be the 'most exact, comprehensive, and plausible "pagan" parallel to Christianity' – and specifically to the 'Christianity of the *Reformation*' (101).[44] Delving in some detail into the Yodo-Shin and Yodo-Shin-Shu movements of twelfth- and thirteenth-century Japan, he concludes that despite their remarkable parallels to Reformation Christianity these traditions do not qualify theologically as true religions. Their very similarity to Protestant Christianity makes it all the more evident that 'among the religions only one thing is decisive concerning truth and falsehood ... *the name Jesus Christ*' (105). Once again the christological concreteness of Barth's thought is evident. He even goes so far as to identify the true religion with the specifically Protestant form of Christianity. Protestant Christianity, he maintains, is worthy of being designated the true religion to the extent – and *only* to the extent – that 'the Reformation was a reminder of the grace and truth summed up in this name'. All the characteristically evangelical doctrines of justification by faith alone, predestination, the sacraments, and so on, have significance 'as symptoms, predicates of the subject Jesus Christ' (106). The christological principle is not reversible: the Christian religion is a religion of grace because it is the religion founded on the name Jesus Christ, but a religion of grace is not automatically a true religion.

The question of a non-Christian religion of grace provides the hinge in Barth's argument that brings it to its culmination and introduces its final movement:

> Therefore: through the grace of God there are men who live by his grace. Or stated concretely: through the name Jesus Christ there are men who have faith in this name. As long as this is the self-understanding of Christians and of the Christian religion, it can and must be said of it that it, and it alone, is the true religion. (108)

The remainder of the section is a kind of denouement, consisting of four parallel meditations on the 'relationship between the name Jesus Christ and the Christian religion', viewed from the respective standpoints of four classic topics of Christian doctrine: creation, election, justification, and sanctification. In each case Barth draws the theological implications and appends an excursus devoted to a specific point related to the doctrinal topic under discussion. Of particular interest to scholars of religion is the first excursus (related to the doctrine of creation), which elaborates the specifically institutional side of the theory of religion. Barth argues that since the Christian religion is 'nothing other than the earthly and historical life of the church and the children of God', it is best thought of as 'an annexe to the human nature of Jesus Christ' (110). The christological concreteness of Barth's thought thus extends not only to religious ideas and teachings but also to the social embodiment of religion in human history and culture.

Barth among the Religionists

How, then, does Karl Barth's theory of religion compare with other influential theories in modern academia? And what light does comparison with Barth shed on those other positions? These are the kinds of questions that *religious studies* ought to be asking. For the past several years, the Department of Religious Studies at Connecticut College has included Barth in its advanced seminar in Theories of Religion, required of all majors and minors. Fresh from their study of works by Durkheim, Eliade, Freud, and James, students are asked to read and analyse Barth's account of the sublimation of religion. Students typically react in surprise, or even outrage, to the obvious 'bias' or 'presuppositions' of the author. This response gives us the opportunity to have them reflect comparatively on the biases and presuppositions of other modern theorists. It soon becomes apparent that many students, like many of the theorists they have been reading, implicitly assume that they can adopt a neutral or 'unbiased' standpoint in studying religious phenomena – an assumption that most of them soon come to recognize as untenable. The outcome is an increasingly sophisticated appreciation of both the inevitability and the importance of the standpoint one adopts in studying religion or any other cultural phenomenon. The very fact that Barth so obviously, and yet explicitly, speaks from a standpoint very different from that of most students helps them to see that other thinkers, too, come to the study of religion with a set of prior commitments, whether 'religious' or otherwise. The invisibility of those commitments in the case of the more secular theorists is the result not of their methodological neutrality but rather of the fact that students today more readily take those commitments for granted.

As we and our students have discovered, comparing Barth's theory of religion with other theoretical positions commonly taught in religious studies leads to some surprising and interesting conclusions. In the first place, Barth's insistence on the *theological* nature of his theory of religion invites comparison with the quite different methodological commitments of other theorists, especially those who have a large stake in the *scientific* nature of their methods. According to Durkheim, for example, 'scientific thought is only a more perfect form of religious thought. Thus,' he concludes, 'it seems natural that the second should progressively retire before the first, as this becomes better fitted to perform the task.'[45] Freud's panegyric to science is even more exuberant. Convinced that 'religion is comparable to a childhood neurosis', he exhorts modern adults to turn instead to science and worship 'Our God, Logos'. The final words of *The Future of an Illusion* proclaim Freud's commitment: 'No, our science is no illusion. But an illusion it would be to suppose that what science cannot give us we can get elsewhere.'[46] The issue thus raised is not simply the difference between a theological and a scientific theory of religion, for Barth, too, insists that his approach is scientific. For Barth, what makes a method scientific is its *Sachlichkeit* – its appropriateness to the object of study.[47] The prominence in the religious studies canon of theorists holding a positivist view of science is one more reminder of the era in which it arose, and a further reason why it needs to be opened up to newer and different voices today.

What is most striking, however, about Barth in comparison with the 'canonical' theorists is how many analytic strategies they hold *in common*. Popular wisdom assumes that theologians will be biased in favour of religion while secular theorists are more likely to be critical. But one is hard pressed to find a non-theological interpreter who makes a more negative value judgment about religion than does Barth. Even at his most descriptive and phenomenological, as we have seen, he portrays religion as an inevitable dialectic of human error and disillusionment. Far from opposing Freud's view of religious ideas as wish-based illusions, Barth in effect agrees (though his reasons are of course very different from Freud's).

On other matters, too, Barth turns out to have strange bedfellows among the secular religionists. One of the issues on which modern theorists of religion have disagreed most sharply concerns the individual versus the social nature of religion. At one extreme is William James, who defines religion as 'the feelings, acts, and experiences of individual men in their solitude, so far as they apprehend themselves to stand in relation to whatever they may consider the divine'.[48] The opposing view is set forth in classic form by Durkheim: 'A religion is a unified system of beliefs and practices relative to sacred things, that is to say, things set apart and forbidden – beliefs and practices which unite into one single moral community called a Church, all those who adhere to them.'[49] In his unstinting emphasis on the corporate and social nature of religion (both in its faithless forms and in response to revelation), Barth stands with Durkheim and the prevailing consensus among twentieth-century social scientists.

Barth's theory of religion poses a challenge to scholars of religion that goes beyond his particular point of view by raising the question of how seriously they are to take their object of study. In our course on Theories of Religion we ask students to imagine positions analogous to Barth's in other religious traditions. Might an Islamic theorist, for example, approach religion from the standpoint of the Qur'an with a methodological rigour like that with which Barth applies the biblical revelation in Jesus Christ? Wilfred Cantwell Smith raises such questions in his intriguing essay 'Is the Qur'an the Word of God?'[50] If scholars of religion are serious about understanding religious traditions, they ought to attend carefully to the unique self-understanding of the representatives of those traditions. Rather than favouring accommodationist theologians like Tillich, who stand self-consciously 'on the boundary' of their tradition, religious studies would do better to attend to those representatives of a tradition who speak with consistency from its central sources of truth.

Challenging the Religious Studies Canon

So why *has* the field of religious studies ignored so fascinating and important an account of religion by one of the twentieth century's leading thinkers? In recent years the academic study of religion, like other disciplines in the humanities and social sciences, has become increasingly sophisticated and self-conscious about the assumptions it makes in carrying out its task. This new awareness concerns not only issues of explicit methodology, something that scholars have long taken seriously, but also the implicit or unconscious biases that inevitably accompany our attempts to understand any aspect of the natural or social world. The impulses driving this change in sensibility come from multiple sources: recent philosophy of science, the sociology of knowledge, and the various forms of the 'hermeneutics of suspicion' that have grown from the seeds sown by such earlier thinkers as Marx, Nietzsche, and Freud.[51] Despite the diversity, and even incompatibility, among the various strands of critique, their cumulative impact has left scholars hypersensitive to the uncriticized values and interests implicated in knowledge. The more politicized versions of these critiques, especially Marxist and feminist ones, are impossible to overlook today; but they are only the most insistent expressions of a wider sea change that can be summed up in the oft-cited motto, originating in philosophy of science, that 'All data are theory laden.' The increasing acceptance of this principle has produced what can be called the postmodern turn in religious studies. I am employing the term 'postmodern' in a modest sense to indicate any theoretical position that eschews the 'modern' assumption of a single, universal order of truth to which one can appeal as a criterion in judging particular claims to knowledge.[52] Postmodern theories, whatever their differences, assume a relativity of perspectives that precludes any possibility of an epistemologically 'pure' or neutral access to truth. Accordingly, a theory may be postmodern in this non-technical sense of the word without necessarily employing that term as part of its self-description. As a result of this postmodern turn, scholars of religion now increasingly take for granted that all expressions of religion – and all theories *about* religion – are socially and historically located and necessarily implicated in paradigmatic commitments to certain values, concepts, and methods.[53]

In spite of the nearly universal acceptance of the postmodern turn in religious studies, however, the field as a whole has so far failed to carry out its implications consistently, especially when it comes to theories about the nature, function, and value of religion. Most scholars of religion will readily agree, for example, that a body of religious doctrines – say, those of the Vedas – reflects the point of view of an all-male priestly elite, or that documents like the New Testament gospels are shaped by the class consciousness and economic status of marginal Jewish sectarians in the Roman Empire. But when we turn from the data of the religions under investigation to the assumptions guiding the modern interpreter of the data, surprising blind spots appear. On the one hand, scholars of religion have been highly sensitive to the unacknowledged religious (usually Christian) bias behind many earlier (and some recent) accounts of religion, and the field of religious studies has worked hard to disentangle itself, both methodologically and institutionally, from religious apologetic interests. On the other hand, it is rare to find the same scrutiny directed towards secular or 'scientific' interpretations of religion. A perusal of course syllabases and textbooks on the theory and methodology of religious studies shows a surprising agreement about the theoretical positions to be included. Social scientific theories predominate, typically classified under the rubrics of anthropology, sociology, and psychology. The theories of Marx, Levi-Strauss, Freud (and sometimes Jung), Durkheim, Geertz, and William James are among the usual selections. History of religions also enjoys a prominent position within the canon of religious studies, invariably represented by Eliade. Some textbooks and courses supplement this list with philosophical theories and methods, typically including logical positivist, process, and existentialist approaches. This last group may include figures identified with religious traditions, such as Tillich or Buber.[54]

A critical analysis of this religious studies canon reveals an unacknowledged inconsistency between the professedly postmodern assumptions of religious studies and the implicit criteria of selection actually at work in the field. We have continued uncritically the legacy of earlier generations of scholars, who, confident that they could distinguish 'objective' or 'descriptive' treatments of religion from those that are 'biased' or 'confessional', established a canon of received theories of religion, in which liberal theologians (like Tillich) were welcome but from which more orthodox theologians (like Barth) were excluded. The perpetuation of this canon, never justifiable on cogent academic grounds, has become an outright embarrassment in the postpositivist and postmodernist environment of the academy today. In a time when most scholars of religion assume the theory-laden nature of all description and the social location of all theories, no credible argument remains for teaching Durkheim, Freud, or Eliade on religion while ignoring Barth and others who speak on the basis of an explicit religious commitment.

One of the temptations implicit in the secular study of religion, evident from its origins in the Enlightenment onward, has been a tendency for it to become the mouthpiece for the post-Christian intelligentsia of European society, a kind of quasi-religion for scholarly non-believers. The anti-religious polemics of many of the earlier and now classic theorists of religion – Durkheim, Freud, Max Müller, and others – make scholars today rather uncomfortable, and the more offensive passages are seldom included in the standard anthologies. Though few scholars of religion today want to claim that the study of religion is incompatible with religious belief,[55] a general attitude of suspicion continues to prevail towards scholars and texts that are either too obvious or too orthodox in their religious commitments. It is this attitude that makes the proposal to take seriously Karl Barth's theory of religion seem so odd to some. The oddity, however, stems not from Barth's ideas but rather from an inherent contradiction within the field of religious studies, brought about by the survival into the postmodern present of a set of theories canonized in the age of modernism.

Not everyone, however, is convinced that the postmodern turn has been good for religious studies. Indeed, the proposal to invite Karl Barth into the canon of theorists of religion has roused the ire of one very vocal critic in particular, Russell T. McCutcheon. In his book *Critics Not Caretakers* he warns of a new and dangerous attempt 'to relegitimize theological discourses in the academy', focusing in particular on 'Garrett Green's odd proposal that Karl Barth's "theory" of religion ought to be included in the religious studies canon'.[56] (McCutcheon cannot bring himself to use the name Karl Barth in the same sentence as 'theory' without putting scare quotes around the latter.) McCutcheon has a very specific – and very narrow – view of what constitutes a proper theory. To count as genuine, he argues, an alleged theory would have to explain the doctrines and practices of a religious or other social community as 'the material products of particular genders, classes, eras, regions, and so on' (147). He is saying, to use Marxist terminology, that all such social doctrines and practices are ideological and therefore suspect and in need of critique. But unlike the classical Marxist theorist, McCutcheon does not think he is engaged in an objective scientific account of the world as it really is, for he repeatedly assures us that he like everybody else has 'all sorts of pretheoretical commitments, aims, and motives, the truth of which can neither be verified nor falsified' (146). But in that case, what protects his own theory from being ideological? When one asks this question, one discovers what can only be called McCutcheon's metaphysical commitments, that is, his pre-theoretical and unverifiable assumptions about what is really real. For, he is saying, even though we too have pre-theoretical commitments, they do not, like religious commitments, 'have ... to do with intentional, invisible agents ... controlling the course of cosmic history' (146). In other words, only philosophical empiricists are to be granted entry into the scholarly study of religion. It's all right to believe in market forces, or social formation, or (presumably) quarks and neutrinos, but not in gods, ghosts, or souls. The problem is not that McCutcheon holds such views – many scholars of religion hold similar metaphysical commitments – but his justification, or rather lack of justification, for making such a value judgment. Some pre-theoretical commitments are evidently more equal than others.

The issue between McCutcheon and other scholars of religion (who surely represent by far the majority, though these matters will not be decided by a vote) concerns the fundamental nature of religious studies as a discipline. McCutcheon represents a viewpoint that can be called neopositivist, comprised of scholars who believe that the academic study of religion is legitimately practised only by social scientists who employ the empirically testable methods of the 'hard' sciences – in other words, by religious outsiders. It is true that the tension between 'outsiders' and 'insiders' has been part of the dynamics of the field since its earliest days. But that tension will not be broken by authoritarian claims by neopositivists who believe that they possess the only valid methodology for the study of religion.

The academic study of religion as we know it today emerged not only out of the anti-religious critiques of the Enlightenment and its naturalist heirs but rather from the interplay of *two* historical movements – what we might call for brevity's sake the outsider and the insider traditions. The very concept of religion, as used in academia and elsewhere in contemporary culture, is a modern invention, rooted in the secularization of European society over the past three centuries. From the seventeenth century onward, Enlightenment critics of religion (which in the European context almost always meant historical Christianity) wanted to distinguish 'natural' religion, assumed to be universal and shared by all human beings, from the revealed or 'positive' religions rooted in history and making claims to particular historical authorities. Their nineteenth-century heirs included many of the founders of the modern study of religion: scholars like Tylor, Fraser, Max Müller, and Durkheim, who make up the bulk of the received religious studies canon. Alongside this 'outsider' tradition, however, there emerged a different but equally important tradition of modern 'insider' reflection on religion, by scholars who sought to articulate, or re-articulate, the truth of traditional Christianity in the context of modern secular culture while resisting naturalist critiques of religion. And with passage of time, Christian scholars have been joined in this enterprise by Jewish, and most recently, Islamic scholars. This insider tradition includes many of the greatest thinkers of modernity, including Kant, Hegel, Schleiermacher, Kierkegaard – and, in the twentieth century, Paul Tillich, Rudolf Bultmann, and Karl Barth. What *both* outsiders *and* insiders have in common is their focus on the modern concept of *religion* as a distinct cultural reality as distinguished from the particular historic religious communities. In other words, both religious outsiders and insiders have long had a stake in the project of identifying, analysing, and evaluating religion. Often, especially in the early days of the discipline, the tension between these two modern traditions erupted into conflict, and there were those on both sides who called for a strict separation of 'religious studies' from 'theology'.

It would have surprised those earlier thinkers, both outsiders and insiders, to see what has emerged from their labours as the field of religious studies in the early twenty-first century. For instead of increasing polarization between 'religion' and 'theology,' we find ourselves engaged in a fascinating and bewilderingly complex academic field in which most of the lines our forebears tried to draw have become obscured, entangled, or erased – much to the dismay of neo-outsider purists like Professor McCutcheon. Not only are religious studies departments inhabited by a robust mix of outsiders and insiders, but many in the field find that the lines of division run not between one group of scholars and another but right through their own minds and souls (*pace* Professor McCutcheon). Religious 'insiders' in the academy – who no longer include just Protestant Christians along with a few Catholics and Jews, but most of the major faiths of the world – are also participants in the emerging global culture of the secular university, and are consequently 'outsiders' as well. And the same can surely be said of most of the students who come to religious studies departments to learn about religion – their own as well as other people's. Surely, in light of this situation, the field of religious studies should strive to be multiperspectival, welcoming all sorts and conditions of outsiders and insiders but also that growing company of hybrids who are in one sense outsiders while in another sense insiders. Lest I be accused of promoting an anything-goes policy in the study of religion, let me hasten to add that there are indeed legitimate limits and criteria for entry into the religious studies guild but they are not constituted by the traditionally contested and questionable distinction between outsiders and insiders. Rather, the academic study of religion ought to be open to any scholar who has the appropriate academic preparation and is also prepared to engage in the *public* discourse about religion, whatever his or her private beliefs and practices might be. This criterion allows for theologians to participate in religious studies, so long as they are willing to do their theologizing 'in public' – that is, in dialogue with, and under the scrutiny of, colleagues who do not necessarily share their own implicit or pre-theoretical commitments. Needless to say, these criteria are not likely to produce a neatly organized and methodologically pure discipline – and that is probably fortunate, whatever the confusions it will inevitably entail. So as a start, let me invite my fellow scholars and students of religion to wade into the fray and find out what Karl Barth *really* said about religion.

On Religion

THE REVELATION OF GOD AS THE SUBLIMATION OF RELIGION

God's revelation in the outpouring of the Holy Spirit is the judging, but also reconciling, presence of God in the world of human religion – that is, in the realm of attempts by man to justify and sanctify himself before a wilfully and arbitrarily devised image of God. The church is the site of the true religion to the extent that through grace it lives by grace.

1. THE PROBLEM OF RELIGION IN THEOLOGY

The event of God's revelation is to be understood and presented here as it is attested to the church of Jesus Christ by the Holy Scripture. This concrete constraint, within which theology has to work, required us in the previous section to give to this question – How is it actual, and how is it possible, that God comes to man in his revelation? – the unambiguous answer that both the *actuality* and the *possibility* of this event are the being and action of God, and in particular of the Holy Spirit. The actuality *and* the possibility! We were able to make the distinction between them only for the sake of clear understanding; and what there was to understand in this case was finally just this: that *both* are to be sought *in God* and only in God. We were thus prevented from finally taking seriously this distinction as such. We were prevented from establishing the actuality of revelation in God but its possibility in man; from attributing the event to God but the agency or point of contact for it to man; from understanding divine grace as the particular feature in this matter but the human appropriation and receptivity as the universal feature. In other words, we were prevented from interpreting God as the matter but man as the form, thereby treating the event of revelation as an interplay between God and man, grace and nature. Rather, because we wished to hold ourselves to Holy Scripture as, for us, the normative witness of revelation, we saw ourselves compelled to conclude that this event – though it is surely an event that happens to man – constitutes a self-enclosed circle; that not only the objective but also the

33

subjective side of revelation, not only its actuality but also its potentiality, is solely the being and action of the self-revealing God himself.

But inasmuch as revelation is in fact an event that also happens to man – an event that also has the form, at least, of human existence, experience, and activity – we come upon the problem of *human religion*. The revelation of God by the Holy Spirit is actual and possible as a determination of human existence. Were we to deny this, how would we then understand it as revelation? But if we do not deny it, we must recognize that it also has at the very least the character and face of a human, historically and psychologically comprehensible phenomenon, into whose nature, structure, and value one may enquire as in the case of other human phenomena – one that can be viewed alongside other human phenomena of a more or less similar kind, and understood and judged accordingly. But the field of enquiry that thereby comes under consideration is precisely that of *religion*. We have tried to present as strictly and consistently as possible the actuality and possibility of revelation, even in its subjective aspect, as divine actuality and possibility. But in doing so, how could we have avoided speaking just as definitely and concretely about an encounter and communion between God and man, about church and sacrament, about a certain being and conduct of man before God? Precisely in so doing, however, we have spoken about human things – which is to say, about things that are no doubt remarkable but are hardly unique – about things astounding but hardly inconceivable, about things of a basically similar kind to what one finds elsewhere as well. Viewed from this aspect, what we call revelation necessarily appears as something particular in the general field that one calls religion – as 'Christianity' or 'Christian religion' – one predicate of a subject that can have other predicates as well, one species in a genus to which other species belong as well. There are, after all, apart from and alongside Christianity, also Judaism and Islam, Buddhism and Shintoism, animistic and totemistic, ascetic, mystical, and prophetic religions of all kinds. Again: we would have to deny revelation as such if we were to dispute the fact that it is also just this – Christianity – that it also has this human face and in this regard stands in a series along with other human faces, that seen from this angle it is surely remarkable but certainly not unique. This fact should be calmly acknowledged, and the idea should be thought calmly through to the end: there is something human by nature, something we can by no means overlook, something we must call by its real name if we wish to recognize and acknowledge God's revelation as revelation – and this human something also exists *beyond* Christianity, *universally*, as a particular realm of human existence, experience, and activity, as one of the worlds within the world of man.[1]

Furthermore, human beings beyond Christianity, universally, also seem to feel, and with some urgency, that they are confronted by certain forces that are superior to their own life and that of the world and that influence it. They seem to know of spirit and of spirits and their effects even at the most primitive stages of their intercourse with nature. Human culture in general and human existence in particular seems always and everywhere to be related to something ultimate and decisive, which is at least a powerful rival to their own will and ability. Culture and existence seem to have been determined or co-determined by a reverence, allegedly transcending man himself, for an Other or even Wholly Other, for a Supreme Relative or even Absolute. Always and everywhere people seem to know of the actuality and possibility of a consecration or even a sanctification of human life on the basis of a striving, experienced individually or communally, which (likewise always and everywhere) is traced back to an event taking place in that Beyond. Moreover, always and everywhere, the representation of the object and goal of this striving, or of the origin of this event, has been concentrated in images of gods, in whose background the image of one sole and supreme God nearly always becomes more or less clearly visible. When and where did people not know of the obligation of human beings to offer worship to God or the gods in the form of concrete cults – whether through intercourse with the images and symbols of divinity; through sacrifice, acts of atonement, and prayers; through customs, games, and mysteries; through the formation of congregations and churches? When and where have people not also thought and claimed they heard the voice of divinity and endeavoured to penetrate its meaning? Is not the Veda to Indians, the Avesta to Persians, the Tripitaka to Buddhists – is not the Qur'an 'the Bible' to its believers in the same way the Old and New Testaments are to us? Are not at least the elements and problems of the world views of all religions – the beginning and end of the world, the origin and nature of man, moral and religious law, sin and redemption – identical with those of Christian doctrine? May we not, and must we not, see *Christian* 'piety' too, even in its highest and finest forms, on a scale with the forms of piety generally, even if perhaps at the highest level? And measured by what criteria would it necessarily be accorded that highest level anyway?

By establishing that all of this really does exist outside and alongside 'Christianity', we are acknowledging that God in his revelation has in fact entered into a sphere in which his actuality and possibility is surrounded by a sea of more or less exact, but at any rate basically unmistakable, parallels and analogies in human actualities and possibilities. God's revelation is in fact God's presence and thus God's *hiddenness* in the world of human *religion*. Because God reveals himself, the divine particular is hidden in a human universal, the divine content in a human form, and thus the *divinely unique* in something merely *humanly remarkable*. One can view God from this side too, and also the outpouring of the Holy Spirit, and certainly also the incarnation of the Word, precisely because and in so far as it is God's revelation to man. That is, in its hiddenness, which is of course given together with its true humanity, one can view the incarnation as a religious phenomenon; as a member of that series; as a special image within a general observation and experience; as the particular content of a human form that can have other contents as well, and in which the divine particularity of that content is not directly recognizable.

We must add here for the sake of clarification that the impression that we are dealing with human *religion* at the place where the church thinks it should speak of God's *revelation* is not more uncertain and weaker but rather more definite and stronger than in other areas of the history of religion. For it is no accident that expositions of the general phenomenology of religion are accustomed to take the most striking examples of the various types of religious formation and action precisely from our Bible (and the history of the Christian church), as though it were itself, as Adolf von Harnack has said, a 'compendium of the history of religion'. If it is true, as Harnack thinks, that whoever knows *this* religion knows them *all*, then it surely cannot be for the reason that it is easier to separate the 'Christian religion' from the world of religion in general than other religions. D. F. Strauss ought at any rate to be heard when he makes this objection to the apologists for the supernatural revealedness of Christianity: 'Because the fruit now lies before us, loosed as ripe fruit is wont to be from the twig and branch that bore it, it is supposed not to have grown on a tree but rather to have fallen directly from heaven. Childish notion! And even if we can show ever so plainly the stalk by which it was attached to the maternal bough; even if its growth obviously shows its unmistakable kinship with other local fruits; even if on its surface we can still see the traces of the sun that irradiated it, or the hailstones that pierced it, or even the prick of wicked insects that attacked it – nevertheless it is supposed to have sprung from no earthly stem, nor have ripened in our atmosphere.'[2]

If one does not wish to deny God's revelation precisely as *revelation*, one will by no means be able to escape the fact that it can also be regarded from a standpoint from which under certain circumstances it may be denied as *God's* revelation. It can, and indeed it must, *also* be understood as 'Christianity' and thus *also* as religion and thus *also* as a human actuality and possibility. Just what this 'also' signifies specifically is to be shown in this section. We must first of all get clear about the question itself that is thereby raised, and what underlies the double possibility of answering it.

The question that is raised by the fact that God's revelation is to be understood also as a religion among religions is basically quite simply the question, once more, whether theology as theology, whether the church as church, and finally whether faith as faith is willing and able to take itself, or rather the ground of itself, seriously. For theology, church, and faith have here an extremely convenient opportunity not to take themselves and their ground seriously. The problem of *religion* – since it is none other than the precise expression of the problem of *man* in his encounter and fellowship with God – is an opportunity to fall into *temptation*. Theology, church, and faith are invited at this point to abandon their theme, their object, thereby becoming hollow and empty, mere shadows of themselves. On the other hand, they have just at this point an opportunity to keep to the subject matter, to become really certain in their view of it, and so to confirm and strengthen themselves as that which they are called. In the decision here indicated it cannot be a question of whether God's revelation is to be understood also as human religion and hence as a religion among religions. We saw that denying this proposition would mean denying the humanity of revelation, and this would mean denying revelation as such. The question, however, is whether this proposition is to be expounded and applied to mean that that which we think we know about the essence and appearance of religion has to serve as the criterion and explanatory principle for God's revelation, or vice versa: whether we have to interpret religion – the Christian religion and all other religions – according to what is said to us by God's revelation. It obviously makes a difference whether religion is *the* problem of *theology* or whether it is *one* problem *in* theology. It makes a difference whether the church is a religious society or in fact a place where even religion is 'sublimated' in the most comprehensive sense of the word. It makes a difference whether faith understands itself as a form of human piety or as a form of the judgment and the grace of God that is, to be sure, always and very concretely related to human piety in all its forms. That is the decision that is meant here.

We touch upon one of the most difficult historical puzzles when we maintain that in modern Protestantism – as it has presented itself from the eighteenth to the twentieth centuries, growing from sixteenth- and seventeenth-century roots – the great definitive decisions have come down on the first side of the oppositions just indicated. It was and is a characteristic of its theological thinking as it occupies us here (in the context of its conception and formulation of church and life) that, in its great representatives and decisive tendencies, it has not viewed and explained religion from the standpoint of revelation but rather revelation from the standpoint of religion.

An epigraph for the following: 'The word *religion* was introduced in most emphatic opposition to the word *faith* as commonly used in the Lutheran, Reformed, and Catholic churches, and always presupposes the Deist critique of the universal Christian concept of revelation. Do we still wish to assert that we are within the sphere of the Reformation?' (Paul de Lagarde, *Deutsche Schriften*, 4th printing, p. 46).

Even if Thomas Aquinas (*Summa theologiae* II/2, q. 81f.) spoke of the universal (moral) virtue of 'religion' and (II/2, q. 186f.) of the specifically monastic 'religion', or if he occasionally designated the object of theology as 'Christian religion' (e.g., in the prologue to the *Summa theologiae*) or as 'religion of faith', obviously the notion of a non-Christian 'religion' nevertheless lay completely outside his horizon: he appears not to have known under this name what we designate by it. Moreover, the concept of religion as a *generic* concept, to which the Christian religion would be subordinated as *one among others*, is obviously utterly foreign to him. In substance the problem was, to be sure, already posed for the Middle Ages by Claudius of Turin, by John Scotus Erigena, and by Abelard. Yet it did not and could not become important until after the Renaissance.

37

But even if Calvin spoke, in the humanist style, of 'Christian religion' right in the title of his *magnum opus*, he surely had not the slightest intention of thereby making 'Christian' into a predicate of something neutrally and universally human. What he describes in the *Institutes* (1.2.2) as 'pure and real religion: faith so joined with an earnest fear of God that this fear also embraces willing reverence, and carries with it such legitimate worship as is prescribed in the law'[3] – that is plainly a normative concept derived from Holy Scripture, in which the universal is sublimated in the particular, hence religion in revelation, and not vice versa. And even if Calvin also attributed to fallen man an inalienable 'seed' of such religion (1.3.1 f.), he nevertheless immediately sets over against it the knowledge that this 'seed' does not come to maturity in a single human being, let alone bear fruit (1.4.1; 12.1). Thus the concept of 'religion' as a universal and neutral form was unable to achieve any fundamental significance for Calvin's conception and presentation of Christianity; rather, 'religion' for him is an entity 'x' that receives its content and its form only through being equated with Christianity – which means, however, that it is taken by revelation into itself and conformed to its pattern.

On the whole, the earlier orthodox theologians (J. Gerhard and L. Hutterus of the Lutherans, Bucan and H. Alting, Gomarus and Voetius, and even J. Coccejus of the Reformed) avoided any systematic treatment or discussion of the concept of religion – but so too among the later orthodox did J. W. Baier on the one side and F. Turrettin and P. V. Mastricht on the other. For Baier, religion is still simply the sum of the possibilities for a 'natural theology' insufficient for the knowledge of salvation, and is neither materially nor formally set in relation to revelation.[4]

Already at the start of the seventeenth century the two Basel theologians Polanus and (his obvious disciple) Wolleb constitute a striking exception. Even in these two, however, the doctrine of religion does not appear among the principles of theological knowledge at the pinnacle of the system but rather (not, perhaps, without dependence on the example of Thomas Aquinas) in ethics, and in fact as the introduction to the explanation of the commandments of the first table, the second through the fourth commandments in particular, and immediately receives its contents, just as in Calvin, as the doctrine of the true religion, that is, the sole and necessary religion founded by God himself, which is identical to the Christian religion, namely, the Christian religion as inwardly apprehended by man.[5] Other than it, there is only false and hypocritical religion and irreligion (pp. 3718f.). For natural man, who is a liar, is incapable of true religion from the standpoint of knowledge as well as from that of the will (p. 3710). 'True religion alone is properly so called; other things are called religion, but they are not' (p. 3697).[6] A free choice between it and other 'religions' cannot therefore come into consideration (p. 3718). Nevertheless, in J. Wolleb a universal neutral definition of the concept religion can even crop up (something Polanus obviously wanted to avoid!), though hidden and rendered harmless by the context: '"Religion" … denotes in its general signification all worship of God, especially the unmediated worship of God, but most especially either the internal worship of God or the internal and external together'[7] – to which the concept of 'true religion'[8] might appear to be subordinated as a species.

But in a Dutch disciple of Polanus, Anton Walaeus,[9] and in the Leiden Synopsis of 1624,[10] the concept of religion does indeed turn up in a quite different and more insidious context, namely, in the arguments for establishing the authority and necessity of Holy Scripture. According to Walaeus, they are supported by the fact that in Holy Scripture the 'true and saving religion' is transmitted, namely, the 'Christian religion' bearing the marks (*notae*) of the 'true and divine religion'. These 'marks' are given as follows: (1) the 'true knowledge of the true God', (2) the 'true reason for the reconciliation of man with God', (3) the 'true worship of God'. We find these 'marks' in the Christian religion taught in the Bible and in no other. In them we recognize the marks of the true religion – and now there occurs something unfortunate – 'the *conscience* of men telling them this':[11] 'nature herself teaches [them] to seek these things in true religion'.[12] And because of them we take the Bible to be of divine origin and hence necessary. No doubt one can take even this quite unambiguous reference to a universal concept of religion, known to us according to the voice of conscience or nature, to be innocuous, because it is supposed to have significance 'only' in connection with arguments for the validity of Holy Scripture directed against the atheists and the papacy, hence 'only' for apologetic intent. But how long, once it has made its appearance, will it have only apologetic significance? Does it not in fact already in Walaeus carry more weight that he himself admits? One has to ask, because in him and in the Leiden Synopsis the very basis for recognizing the divinity of Holy Scripture, which for Calvin[13] was the one and only, beside which *all* other arguments came into consideration only as 'secondary aids to our feebleness'[14] (definitely not, by the way, an argument 'from true religion'!) – namely, the 'internal testimony of the Holy Spirit' – plays an appallingly incidental role. Does that recognition not rest, after all, far more on those arguments and hence – something that does relate to the 'argument from true religion' – on a universal concept of religion known to us through conscience and nature? And what difference will that make for the exposition and application of Holy Scripture? For Walaeus and the Leiden theologians in fact it still doesn't make much difference. But we can nevertheless clearly foresee here what a difference it is going to make one day.

Very peculiar is the position of Abraham Heidan,[15] who (like many of his theological contemporaries, especially in Holland) clearly had the intention of uniting Calvin and Descartes but just as clearly succeeded (to the salvation of his Calvinist components!) only by means of some most remarkable juxtapositions. One cannot emphasize more strongly than he did the foundation of faith and theology on revelation. 'Since religion is the right worship of God, and this consists in a true sense of God and a right affection toward him, and this neither can nor may be reached by us, and is nothing brought to birth by our cleverness, it ought to be decreed for us by God himself, for whom this worship is to be kept. For he alone is the appropriate witness about himself [see Calvin, *Institutes* 1. 7. 4!], who, because it is pleasing to him, is able to teach us, and to whom nothing can be pleasing, unless it is effected by him and fitting to his nature. What that is, no one knows except himself. And how could it become known, unless it should be made plain and revealed to us by himself?' (p. 7f.) One might think that a universal concept of religion would be impossible from this position. But then Heidan recalls the atheists of his day, and soon his Cartesian heart begins to beat: there is a 'natural knowledge of God, which is inborn in individual human beings' (p. 8). Were this not so, how could it become reality in us through tradition and instruction? (p. 9). The existence of God can be proved a priori by way of the ontological argument (p. 11). 'When I contemplate God, I conceived a being most perfect, a divinity most powerful, most wise ...' (p. 12). And: 'from this account of God religion has its rise' (p. 13). The universal concept of religion appears to have been achieved! But now Calvin bestirs himself again, and out it goes. The conclusion that 'right reason should have been the norm of the first religion' is indignantly rejected; even Adam had in fact known God only through revelation (p. 13). 'God cannot be conceived without his word.' Without revelation we would not know of him at all (p. 14). 'This right reason is a mere chimera, a fiction of the human mind' (p. 15). Evidently here too the appearance of that universal concept was an apologetic interlude. As soon as he stops thinking about the atheists, Heidan once again speaks wholly as a theologian of revelation. It is worth noting that in his doctrine of holy scripture he made no use of the 'argument from true religion'. Thus in his case too the coming novelty had only been heralded. He obviously knew how to avoid feeling the contradictions in which he was enmeshed as contradictions in his own person. But it is clear that the problem could not remain at this stage.

It signified an important and dubious step forward when M. F. Wendelin[16] tried to distinguish the 'true religion' as the 'subject of theology' from God as its 'principal efficient cause' and from holy scripture as its 'instrumental efficient cause', and to place it as a formal concept at the pinnacle of the theological system. How did it come about that this matter, which is hardly touched upon in most of the older theologians, which neither in the ethics of Polan and Wolleb nor in the doctrine of holy scripture of Walaeus is referred to as one 'argument' alongside of others – how did this matter advance to such a position? Now to be sure Wendelin is not guilty of filling out the concept of 'true religion' with material from 'conscience' and 'nature', nor did he introduce it as an apologetic moment into his doctrine of scripture. In him, rather, this concept is filled out quite objectively and Christianly. 'True religion' is the 'the way of knowing and honouring God *prescribed by God* for the salvation of man and the glory of God' or the 'complete and entirely godly norm, *authenticated in the sacred writings*, for knowing and honouring God'; it is to this extent 'something divine and infallible, from which no one has the right of appeal'. It is, as Wendelin obviously means, God's revelation in its subjective reality. One may ask why and to what end this particular notion is so emphasized – just as in the case of the hymns of that era. But it is still characterized and emphasized as God's revelation, so that here too the secret misfortune has at least not come to light.

The same can still be said of F. Burmann. But now even more striking accents are becoming visible: the dubious aspects of Walaeus and those of Wendelin, namely, the apologetic rationalizing of the concept of religion on the one hand, and systematic over-emphasis on the other, appear to intensify in him. Differently from his teacher Coccejus, Burmann begins his *Synopsis of Theology* (1678) with a long chapter 'On Religion and Theology', in which once again the concept of the 'rational creature', striving after God but only reaching God through God, stands at the pinnacle (I 2, 1). Again we hear the definition: 'religion' is the 'way of knowing and honouring God', but now in place of the addendum explicitly referring to revelation – 'prescribed by God' or 'authenticated in the sacred writings' – an ambiguous *'correct'* has appeared (2. 4). And it can now be said of this 'religion' as 'the correct way of knowing and honouring God': *'it flows from the nature of God and man itself,* since nothing so befits the rational creature as ... to honour and revere the excellence and highest virtues of God. *Hence religion is a necessary and natural sequel of reason; and therefore there is such a thing as natural religion'* (2, 6–7). But the consequences that could follow here and apparently had to follow, were not yet drawn by Burmann: according to him too this rational religion of the sinner does not achieve its goal for the reason that he is a sinner (2, 11): 'true religion depends on God alone and his revelation', and only the 'Christian religion' is 'true religion' (2, 19). It can be recognized as 'true' because it bears the marks of the true religion; for it gives us the 'true medium' and the 'true way' for communion with God (2, 18). We already heard much the same from Walaeus. In contrast to Walaeus, Burmann at this point did not refer expressly to conscience or to nature as the source of these 'marks'. But neither did he like Wendelin refer expressly to holy scripture. In any event, in his case too one may still console oneself with the explanation, 'To this religion alone is one therefore to adhere' (2, 29) – and with the fact that from this point on his *Synopsis* proceeds fairly straightforwardly as a theology of revelation and scripture.

Meanwhile on the Lutheran side quite similar developments appear to have been taking place. Even in the representatives of Lutheran high orthodoxy in the second half of the seventeenth century (with the exception of Baier)[17] we encounter a chapter 'On the Christian Religion', which is characterized as the 'general subject of theology' and takes systematic precedence over holy scripture as the 'first principle of theological knowledge'. Here too it is in fact theoretically and practically only a matter of the 'Christian religion' with respect to the 'paradisical religion' of Adam before the fall. It is still expressly declared that the concept 'religion' may also be applied only 'improperly, wrongly, and unlawfully' to the worship of God by the pagans, Turks, and Jews, or even by the Roman Catholics. The concept 'religion' is still filled, theoretically and practically, only by holy scripture – or, put more cautiously, by what one takes to be Christian. 'True religion' and 'false religion', or better, 'religion' and 'superstition', still seem to oppose one another like heaven and earth. Here too one will recognize in the entity signified by 'Christian religion' that which we call the subjective reality of revelation. It is striking that this entity in particular emerges so prominently into the foreground, that it is now an independent object of interest, and even more striking that the treatment – in Calov, for example – of the dangerous problem 'Whether the Christian religion is true' now hovers strangely between spiritual and worldly argumentation.[18] But even here one cannot point to a single passage where that line of Calvin's is abandoned in any notorious fashion. More or less parallel to Burmann on the Lutheran side, one could mention David Hollaz.[19] His corresponding chapter is headed 'On Religion and the Articles of Faith' (Prol. 2). He also devotes two whole questions to a universal concept of religion. And like Burmann in contrast to Wendelin, in the definition of 'Christian religion' as 'a way of honouring God', he omits the supplementary phrase 'prescribed by God', unlike Calov, König, and Quenstedt. Instead, the statement of his predecessors that this 'way' consists crucially in faith in Christ is enriched in his case by the addition of 'the sincere love of God and neighbor'. Hollaz is one of the last and strictest representatives of the theory of verbal inspiration and is thus theoretically a scriptural theologian. The Bible was nevertheless not important enough to him for him even to mention it, right at this point where mention of it had such fundamental significance! So powerful, evidently, was the concern which at that time was about to make itself independent, and then superior, under the rubric 'religion'. Still, at the pinnacle of his subsequent definition of 'true religion' (more clearly than in the cases of Walaeus and Burmann) stands the proviso 'which is conformed to the divine Word'. And there can be no doubt that he in fact discerns the only true religion in that religion erected on the foundation of Jesus Christ (identical for him with the 'evangelical religion, which received its name from the ministry of Luther'!).

In this as in other matters, the catastrophe occurred and Neoprotestantism had its true and public birth in the modern movement of so-called rational orthodoxy at the start of the eighteenth century. We can illustrate the development in the Reformed theologian Salomon van Til (1643–1713; *Compendium of Theology Both Natural and Revealed*, 1704) and in the Lutheran J. Franz Buddeus (1667–1729; *Institutes of Dogmatic Theology*, 1724). Buddeus followed the system of Baier in form. But what a difference in substance will become visible precisely in the question at hand! The dogmatics now begins quite openly and candidly – in van Til a 'Natural Theology', amounting to a complete dogmatics, has even been placed up front as an independent first part – by presupposing the concept and describing a universal, natural, and neutral 'religion' which, as 'religion regarded in itself', is the presupposition of all religions. 'For since man has from nature what he has been provided with by reason, that he knows both that God exists and that he ought to duly honour him, he ought to bring forward no less than what he has received from nature itself' (Buddeus I 1, 3). The knowledge of God *follows from* the aptitude of reason? Van Til, as a resolute Cartesian, appears to want to go even a step further by declaring: 'The *first principle* – from which natural religion, as far as a certain demonstration of God and his worship, ought to be drawn up – *is the very light of reason*, discerned in the human mind by implanted, common notions, such that no one very attentive and liberated from prejudices can ignore it' (*Prael.* 4, 1). The definition of this 'natural religion' runs as follows: It is that 'certain human zeal, by which anyone, by the benefit of his own judgment, keeps his own faculties so occupied in the contemplation and observation of the certain light, as he himself finds suitable, that he in whatever case renders that divinity favourable to himself' (*Prael.* 2, 1). On the basis of this 'natural religion' man knows, according to Buddeus (I 1, 5–13), of a supreme being ('a most perfect being, which we call God'), who perfectly unites in himself knowledge, wisdom, and freedom, who is the eternal and almighty, the good and at the same time just, true, and holy in the superlative, the final cause and the governing principle in all, one unique of his kind, to whom we owe obedience and accountability, who opens to us the prospect of an immortal life of the soul and reward in the hereafter, without whose love we cannot be happy, because he alone is the highest good, who wishes to be honoured by us in works, words, and thoughts, who lays upon us certain duties towards ourselves, towards our fellow men, and finally towards him, God himself. The broad development of this natural theology – in a doctrine of God's nature and attributes, of creation and providence, of the moral law of nature, of the immortality of the soul, and even of sin – comprises for van Til the first part of his compendium. And man can know all of this 'easily' (Buddeus I 1, 5)! 'Since reason brightly teaches all human beings, these things have been so ordered together, that, if anyone is able in the use of reason, and is provided with a sound mind, when he first understands these things, he is immediately constrained to give his assent' (I 1, 14). Buddeus, to be sure, is unwilling to allow man a substantial 'internal word' or 'light', as many a mystic had taught, i.e., he will in no way formally assert the existence of a second source of revelation (I 1, 15). Nor does van Til really want to do this directly; in the 'Dedication' of his work, at any rate, he warns young theologians, 'lest the principle of reason occupy the same place as the principle of faith', because the two do not have the same evidence. But what about that 'first knowledge', that original knowledge of man about himself and God, which he does in fact designate and describe as the presupposition of natural religion (*Prael.* 3)? To what extent must and can this knowledge, once asserted, be less convincing than that of revelation? However that may be, Buddeus at least does not forget to make at once the familiar reservation of all representatives of a natural theology: that this 'natural religion' and its knowledge of God does not suffice to attain eternal salvation, because with all those insights man still has not been given the means for fellowship with God, the supreme good, and the right use of this means. He also points to the indispensable completion of that 'natural religion' by revelation (I 1, 16–18). This reservation also belatedly becomes evident in van Til, namely, towards the end of the first and beginning of the second part of his compendium. Yet in spite of this reservation, according to Buddeus, one can say of that 'natural religion': it contains the '*notions*' that are the '*bases and foundations of all religion*' by which man must let himself be measured with regard to his religion, and on the basis of which we are able to recognize the 'religions that rest on revelation' as such. Whatever contradicts these 'notions' of 'natural religion' is either not revelation at all or else misunderstood revelation. 'Natural religion', according to Buddeus, performs for us a double pedagogical service: by its insufficiency, which lets us see the *necessity* of revelation, and by the hint it gives us for finding *true* revelation. It and true revelation – so Buddeus believes he can promise us – never contradict but always correspond to one another (I 1, 19–20). And natural theology culminates in van Til in a doctrine 'On the Preparation for the Gospel', in which (1) from the presuppositions and data of natural religion there is postulated the necessity of a reconciliation between God and man that is not yet given in natural religion as such; (2) again, from the principles of natural religion the conditions of such a reconciliation are given; and finally (3) the pagan, Jewish, Mohammedan, and Christian religions are compared, with the result that the last corresponds to the given conditions and is thus to be recognized as the revealed religion. 'According to the dictates of this rationality, natural theology … searches out whatever religions, in order that you should therefore find out that the Christian religion (although it knows mysteries exceeding the limits of natural science) accords more than the others with the light of nature' ('Preface to the Reader'). That is the programme that was initiated by van Til and Buddeus and carried out to the extent of their abilities (for the first time in the sphere of Protestantism without provoking complaints of impiety).

What took place here (in a turn of events that basically all the leading theologians of the time went along with) cannot be taken seriously enough in its basic significance and its grave historical consequences. In these theologians there emerged clearly and consistently something that had in fact perhaps been to a large extent the secret goal and passion of the whole previous development: human religion, the relationship to God that man can and in fact does have even without revelation, is by no means an unknown quantity, but rather one that is extremely well known in form and content, one that as such is most interesting and of central importance for all theological thinking. It constitutes, namely, the presupposition, the criterion, the necessary framework for understanding revelation. It represents the question answered not only by the other positive religions but also by the religion of revelation, and the Christian religion as its most adequate answer deserves precedence over the others and hence also its characterization as religion of revelation. 'Christian' has now become in fact – the new theological point of departure that had suggested itself so strongly since the Renaissance is now a reality – a predicate of the neutrally and universally 'human', and revelation has become the confirmation of what man can know even without revelation about himself and hence about God. 'The light of nature goes still further. It also discloses to me the true marks of this revelation. No revelation is true unless it accord with the light of nature and augment it ... a true revelation must prove itself as such in my heart through a divine power and conviction which I plainly feel ... which the light of nature teaches, and thus instructs me and makes me eager to seek and to challenge such a revelation and to test the true religion accordingly.'[20]

It is unnecessary for us at this point to unfold in detail the whole further sad story of recent Protestant theology. Buddeus and van Til, whom we have used here as examples, and also the other leading theologians of that generation (Chr. Matth. Pfaff, S. Werenfels, J. A. Turrettin, J. F. Osterwald, J. L. von Mosheim) were recognized not only as serious and pious men but in particular as decidedly conservative ones as well, who, belatedly at least, seem to have known how to do justice to revelation in their theology. They thought they saw the Bible and traditional dogma in nearly full agreement with those postulates of 'natural religion' and the ensuing claims on a truly revealed religion. Thus materially at any rate they did not deviate markedly from the course of orthodoxy in the seventeenth century. They were still very far from that dangerous stabilizing of the relationship of reason and revelation that was soon to appear under the influence of the philosophy of Christian Wolff, which consisted in the idea that basically both are equally convincing, but that they should mutually guarantee their right of ownership as well as their peaceful intercourse in an intermediate sphere common to both. And only after this untenable temporary solution did there follow in the second half of the eighteenth century the ventures of the so-called *Neologians*, who could not convince themselves that all, or even most, of what had hitherto counted as revelation would be able to hold out before that critical authority, and who therefore thought it proper to subject Christian dogma and also the Bible to a very radical critique on the basis of the 'notions' of 'natural religion'. Only then did there follow Kantian *rationalism*, which, taking over from the neologians, reduced 'natural religion' to a 'natural ethics' and tried to interpret revelation as finally no more than the actualization of the moral power of reason. Then Schleiermacher, conversely, wanted to find in religion, understood as feeling, the essence of theology and to find revelation in

44

a particular feeling, hence he wanted to find a particular impression producing a particular religion. And then according to Hegel and D. F. Strauss, the Christian religion along with natural religion is supposed to constitute only a preliminary form, to be sublimated into the absolute knowledge of philosophy, purified of imagination. Then according to L. Feuerbach there is supposed to be nothing at all except natural religion as the illusionary expression of the natural longings and wishes of the human heart. Then A. Ritschl taught that the Christian religion is to be understood as revealed and as true because in it the highest value of human life – namely (the opposite of Feuerbach!), his liberation from the world understood as sensuous nature – is most perfectly realized. Then E. Troeltsch informed us that the theologian should above all practise 'hypothetical empathy' with the phenomena of the universal history of religions, in order then by a comparative appraisal of the various religious worlds to come to the conclusion that Christianity is still the relatively best religion for the time being, and probably for all conceivable times (barring perhaps the arrival of a new ice age!). And only then, finally and at last, was it possible to reach that tumultuous breakthrough of natural religion into the realm of church and theology whose astonished witnesses we have become in our own day. Of course, the worthy van Til and the equally worthy Buddeus could not possibly have dreamed of all this from afar! Even so, they and their generation are to be identified as the true fathers of that Neoprotestant theology which, while not unprepared by the Reformation tradition, nevertheless stands in sharp contrast to it. All of those more or less radical and destructive forms in the history of theology of the last two hundred years have indeed only been variations on a single theme first sounded plainly by van Til and Buddeus: religion is an independent known quantity over against revelation, and *religion is not to be understood from the point of view of revelation, but rather revelation from that of religion.* The intentions and programmes of all the significant movements of modern theology can basically be reduced to this common denominator. Neoprotestantism means 'religionism'. The conservative theology of these centuries, too – the supernaturalist theology of the eighteenth century and the confessional, biblicistic, and 'positive' theology of the nineteenth and twentieth centuries – on the whole went along, making at any rate such concessions to the basic prevailing outlook that, in spite of all the inherent resistance it offered, it cannot be seen as a renewal of the Reformation tradition. Even Christoph Ernst Luthardt (*Compendium of Dogmatics*, 1865, § 2) calmly came to terms with the idea that theology since the eighteenth century is 'science of religion': 'science of Christianity in the sense of the church as the locus of Christianity' – nothing more! And Reinhold Seeberg remarks most calmly at the end of the foreword to the first volume of his dogmatics (1925) that one might ask whether he wouldn't have done better to have written, instead of a dogmatics, a 'philosophy of religion'. But, he continues, interested philosophers and historians, without sharing his particular theological presuppositions, will certainly understand it in just this way. One must regard such an utterance, all things considered, to be symptomatically more significant and alarming than the worst pages in the books of a Strauss or a Feuerbach. It shows that theology at the end of the period that began with Buddeus was really at the point of no longer taking itself seriously as theology.

Why is this development to be judged *negatively*, as a *disturbance* of the life of the church, as finally an actual *heresy* that is fracturing the church? Those who carried out this development – the major and, along with them, countless minor theologians of Neoprotestantism – have always felt themselves to be the dutiful representatives of a *free investigation of truth*, in the face of all mere tradition and its anxieties, even in relation to God and divine things – indeed, they have felt themselves authorized and commissioned. And those who protested more or less firmly against them demonstrated the merely immanent character of their protest, by the fact that on the whole they simply wished to go along to a lesser degree with the consequences of that reversal of revelation and religion; they demonstrated that they themselves stood in the midst of that development, but just less consistently. From the standpoint of a merely conservative opinion and attitude there was and is nothing serious to object to and nothing to be done against that development. Even in the field of theology there is simply *nothing* to be said against the principle of free investigation of truth, and anyone who opposes it will inevitably and rightly cut a sorry figure, as has been shown again and again in the last two hundred years of theological history. Even if in respect of this development he should really represent the concern of the church, he is a poor – a dangerous – representative of this concern; and the question of whether he really intends the interest of the church and is not just following the crowd can never be put to him too sharply from case to case. The motive for opposing that reversal must not be fear of its consequences.

> Thus *not* fear of that dismantling of dogma and biblical teaching, as was carried out in the eighteenth century by wielding the criterion of 'natural religion'; *not* fear of Kant's moralism or Schleiermacher's theology of feeling, of Feuerbach's illusionism, of the biblical criticism of a D. F. Strauss or an F. C. Baur, of a Harnack or a Bousset, of the relativism of the history-of-religions school, etc.! These and many more are indeed possible and actual consequences of that reversal – and, in spite of the already venerable age of some of them, ever recurring consequences. But one cannot shun and reject such consequences unless it is fully clear that one is not participating oneself in that reversal of revelation and religion. To speak quite concretely, one is defenseless against the 'German Christians'[21] of today, unless one has already lodged a well-founded protest against the change of direction in van Til and Buddeus and even earlier – in this case already in König and Quenstedt, in Wendelin and Burmann.

If one does not know this, then one will oppose merely in specific and not in general, not out of knowledge but out of conservatism, that is, out of fear; and then one has lost, even if one means well in each specific case, and even if one achieves all kinds of victories. What serves and helps the church is not this or that mitigation or moderation of the heresy that has penetrated it but rather recognizing, combating, and eliminating it completely. If those feared consequences of the reversal of revelation and religion could really be addressed as possible results of the free investigation of theological truth, then however novel and dangerous they might appear to be, they would have to be tolerated by the church as good and necessary opinions, or at least as ones worthy of discussion and not disruptive of the church community. They can and may and must be opposed – fundamentally and seriously – not because of their novelty and dangerousness, but only because in actual fact they are *not* results of the free investigation of theological truth at all. The opposition must be directed against the point at which those results arise and emerge – not against the free investigation of truth, but rather for the sake of the free investigation of truth. But the point at which such results arise and emerge is an uncertainty in the conception of revelation and of the relationship of God and man determined by it – which simply means an uncertainty or lack of faith. If there is any way at all to explain that historical development, then it must be said – with all the care and reserve requisite in such a judgment – that Protestant theology would never have been able to come up with the thought of that reversal of the relationship of revelation and reason if it, along with virtually the entire church of its time, had not become irresolute concerning something that the Reformers so clearly perceived and recognized: namely, that in Jesus Christ once and for all and in every respect the decision about man has been taken; that Jesus Christ is indeed his Lord, to the end that he, man, might be his own and might live under him and serve him in his kingdom; and that he might therefore have his only consolation in life and in death in the fact that he is not his own possession but Jesus Christ's. To be sure, the Neoprotestant theologians said that too. Indeed, for the most part they left the Reformation confession 'untouched'. The older Protestant theologians, on the other hand, did not leave it untouched but rather made use of it; that is, when they pursued theology they thought, or at least tried to think, in accordance with it. They steadfastly counted on the fact that things were just as it said in the confession, and they did not figure that things might in fact be partially otherwise. For just that reason their theology, that of the Reformers and basically that of the entire older Protestantism as well, was free investigation of truth. For that meant that their theological thinking could be and remain free as such, free for its own inexhaustible object; that it could with him remain true to itself and did not need to be attracted, disturbed, or taken captive by any other points of view. Their theological thinking had the freedom of unconditional objectivity:[22] the freedom of faith, we must say, because this unconditional objectivity was none other than the objectivity of faith. Certainly one cannot and must not blame later theology for the fact that the problem of human religion – more broadly we can say the problem of man in general – came into view and claimed its attention. The period from the sixteenth to the eighteenth centuries was after all in its own way the great period in which European man, taking up

47

again a mighty attempt that Greco-Roman antiquity had already initiated, began to discover himself as man: his essence, his possibilities and capabilities, his humanity. The discovery of the entity 'religion' certainly belonged to this development as well. It is hardly conceivable that theology would not have participated in this discovery.

> To that extent one can give only partial approval to the tendency of the older orthodoxy to pay no attention at all to the problem of religion. At any rate it is testimony to the superiority of Calvin's theology that he was able calmly to incorporate it into his deliberation and exposition. And if the development in the seventeenth and eighteenth centuries had been only a testimony to the fact that Protestant theologians were sufficiently openly involved in the spiritual movement of their time, then one could only affirm it.

Ignorantly or stubbornly to ignore the cares and hopes of the immediate present is really not what is expected or required of theology for the sake of the church. But it is one thing to be open to the concerns, or even to the demonic power, of a particular age and something else to make its concerns one's own, to surrender to its demonic power. The latter is what theology must not do but what it began to do in the seventeenth century and did openly in the eighteenth. It fell prey to the absolutism by which the man of that age made himself the centre, measure, and end of all things. Theology should have compassionately and affectionately observed this trend but by no means joined it; but it followed the trend when in the days of Buddeüs it became openly 'religionistic'. But what was really serious was not what theology did positively but rather what it did *not* do, namely, its negligence, its vacillation in the objectivity of faith: that in this period it stopped treating the cardinal propositions of the Lutheran and the Heidelberg Catechisms as axioms in fact and in practice. Here too the sin was originally and properly *faithlessness*, the neglect of Christ that begins right at the point where one no longer allows him to be the one and all, the secret dissatisfaction with his lordship and consolation. The fact is that this later theology, without denying those propositions of the catechisms, nevertheless thought it could take man seriously from a point of view other than that of the kingdom and possession of Christ. The fact is that this theology could allow its own piety, as distinguished from the word of God spoken to man, to become a special chapter preceding it, and that this chapter could become independent, nay dominant, and in the long run could for its part gradually swallow up the chapter about the word of God. All of this resulted inevitably from that negation, from that omission in the objectivity of faith. So the real catastrophe of modern Protestant theology was not what has so often been represented: that it increasingly retreated in the face of the growing self-consciousness of modern culture; that it unknowingly allowed itself to be instructed from without – from philosophy, from the natural and historical sciences – about what the 'free investigation of truth' really meant; that without realizing it it became something like a rather inconsequential worldly wisdom. Rather, its catastrophe – without which the modern world view, the modern self-conception of man, etc., would not have been able to harm it – was this: that it lost its object, revelation, in its particularity and with it the mustard seed of faith by which it could have moved mountains, even the mountain of modern humanistic culture. That it really lost revelation is shown by the very fact that it was possible for it to exchange revelation, and thereby its own birthright, for the concept of religion.

It always indicates a crucial misunderstanding if one even tries to classify revelation and religion systematically, that is, to juxtapose them as comparable spheres, to mark them off from each other, and to set them in relationship to one another. One's intention and purpose in so doing may be to think from the standpoint of religion and therefore of man, thus subordinating revelation to religion and perhaps even letting it finally be absorbed into it. Or one's intention and purpose may be the opposite: to secure the independence, or indeed the precedence, of the sphere of revelation by means of particular reservations and protections. But that is a secondary question, and for all the variety of possible solutions, *not* a decisive one. If one finds oneself in a position to take human religion seriously on the same level and in the same sense as divine revelation, and thus in some sense to see it as a second something alongside it, to grant it an independent essence and legitimacy over against revelation, even to ask about a balance and relation between these two entities – one who thinks in this way thereby demonstrates that he already has the intention and purpose of thinking from the standpoint of man and not of revelation. And anything one may say later, within the systematic framework so conceived, for the purpose of emphasizing the necessity and reality of revelation can be only a melancholy reminder of the war that was already lost at the outset, or else an actual covering up of the real state of affairs. So it would actually be more desirable, because more instructive, simply to accept the consequences of that point of departure and to refrain from those belated efforts on behalf of revelation. For wherever one tries to compare or reconcile revelation with religion, one has misunderstood it as revelation. Within the context of the problem we are considering, it can only be understood where from the outset, and without any possibility that things could in any way be otherwise, we take into account its *superiority* over human religion, a superiority such that we are not allowed to envisage religion as an object at all from any other standpoint than that of revelation, far less to make statements about its essence and value and thus to allow it to become an independent problem for us. Revelation is understood only where the first and last word about religion is expected from it and from it alone. The question about the problem of religion in theology involves an either/or, from which the slightest deviation, the tiniest concession to religionism, at once makes the correct answer *utterly* impossible.

> One may indeed ask whether this is not much more clearly seen from the diametrically opposite side, namely by the strict representatives of a pure – but *really* pure! – 'science of religion' than by those theologians who orient themselves and their work 'scientifically'.[23] For a 'pure' science of religion, that is, one that really has no pretensions, 'revelation' can only be, after all, either (1) the phenomenon that pops up somewhere in most religions by which they attribute their cultic, mythic, and moral elements to the activity, communication, and ordering of the deity; or (2) the limit concept of truth, beyond and within the plenitude of all the religious realities, which is to be strictly bracketed and not touched upon by the science of religion as such, much less filled out concretely. It would surely be too much to say even that the concept of revelation were respected in this procedure; for true respect would necessarily entail a quite different procedure. The 'purer' the science of religion becomes, the more likely it is to reduce itself to absurdity by drowning in that sea of religious realities (among which there is to be found in abundance and quite explicitly the phenomenon of alleged revelations). Nevertheless, viewed from the standpoint of theology, its procedure must be described as neater, more instructive, and more promising than that mixed science of religion of the theologians, who, on the one hand, are given to disturbing the peaceful course of investigation of religious realities by suddenly appealing to a religious *truth* of revelation; and who yet, on the other hand, by the philosophical standards of judgment and value they apply, betray the fact that they are thereby dealing with a matter that they are in no position to understand and to take seriously.

One who speaks seriously about revelation speaks in the manner of those passages in the catechisms: for him it concerns Jesus Christ the Lord, and therefore man, for whom revelation is intended, because he lives under him and serves him, because he does not belong to himself but to Jesus Christ, and because for that reason he is his sole consolation in life and in death. Whoever deviates even a hair's breadth from this position is not theologically serious, and so is not speaking about revelation at all. Revelation is God's sovereign dealing with man or it is not revelation. The concept 'sovereign' already indicates – and we may presuppose this as 'self-evident' (though not at all self-evident!) in the context of our doctrine of the Holy Spirit – that God is by no means alone in so dealing, and that therefore, if revelation is to be understood, man must by no means be overlooked or excluded. And the same goes for religion as well, whether we mean the Christian religion in particular or human religion in general, to which the Christian also belongs. We are most certainly forbidden, however, to try to know and define and evaluate man and his religion as it were in advance and by itself – in another existence than as belonging to Christ, in another realm than his kingdom, in another relation than 'under him' – in order then, taking it seriously in this autonomous form, to bring it into relationship with God's revelation. For by so doing we would have been saying from the outset that Jesus Christ is not his Lord – not, at least, in the sense of those passages from the catechisms – and that he does not belong to Jesus Christ. We would therefore have denied revelation – for revelation is denied wherever it is treated as problematic – and we would therefore not have spoken of revelation at all in that juxtaposition, however seriously and clearly and emphatically we may have afterwards tried to do so by our words. One must always have spoken about revelation in advance if one really intends afterwards to speak about *it* and not about something altogether different. If one speaks about it only afterwards, then one is speaking, for example, about a postulate or about an idea. What one is then really and truly speaking about is not revelation but rather what came before: man and his religion, about which one thought he already knew so much in advance and did not intend to surrender. There one has his love, his interest, there his zeal, there his trust, there his consolation; and where one has his consolation, there one has his God. *Nothing* can be altered afterwards if one comes to speak of revelation only *afterwards*! If revelation is *not* to be denied but rather believed, and therefore man and his religion understood from the standpoint of those passages from the catechism, then the man to be taken seriously and his religion are precisely not to be sought in that previously established figure. A *systematic* coordination of God and man, of revelation and religion, is therefore out of the question, for the simple reason that the latter – in its own existence as well as its relation to the former – cannot even be viewed, let alone defined, except from the standpoint of the former. Only one thing can be considered, namely, telling the *story* that is enacted between the former and the latter – and enacted in such a way that whatever there is to be said about the existence, nature, and value of the latter becomes visible simply and exclusively in the light of the former, and therefore in the course of God's sovereign dealing with man. The man who becomes visible in the light of revelation, and he *alone*, is the man to be taken seriously. And so likewise the problem of religion in theology is not the question of how the reality 'religion', as defined in advance and in general and therefore untheologically, is to be set in an orderly and plausible relation to the theological concepts of revelation, faith, etc. Rather, without interrupting the theological inquiry, it is the question of what sort of thing it might be that becomes visible from the standpoint of faith as religion in human reality.

The viewpoint by which one must orient oneself in this matter, in order to remain in the analogy of faith and not succumb to untheological thinking, is the *christological*, concerning the incarnation of the Word as the assumption of the flesh. Just as the unity of God and man in Jesus Christ is the unity of a completed *event*, so also the unity of divine revelation and human religion is that of an event – albeit, in contrast to the former, a yet-to-be-completed event. Just

51

as in the former case *God* is the subject of this event, so it is in the latter case as well. Just as in the former case the man Jesus does not already exist in advance and abstractly but only *in the unity* of that event whose subject is the Word of God and thus God himself – true God and true man – so in the latter case the man with his religion is to be viewed strictly as the man who follows God, because God precedes the one who hears God, because he is addressed by God and therefore exists for us only in his capacity as the counterpart of God. One can understand the attitude of the older Protestant theology as distinguished from the newer simply and as it were technically – if one hesitates to attribute it to that deep-seated difference of faith – in this way: they praised Christ and honoured him not only in words, as did the newer theology also in its own way, but rather they knew how to show him praise and honour in deed – namely, in the actual ordering of their thinking about God. In other words, the discipline of the christological dogma of the early church was still a significant presupposition for them, both self-evident and practical. It is understandable, on the other hand, why the christological dogma had to become alien and incomprehensible to the newer theology once it had ceased to be the practical presupposition of their actual thinking.

We can sum up in these words: we have nothing to delete or retract from the recognition that in his revelation God is present in the midst of the world of human religion. But it is important to see what it means to say that *God* is present. It is basically a matter of re-establishing the order of the concepts revelation and religion in such a way that the relation between them becomes comprehensible again as identical with that event between God and man in which God is *God* – that is, the Lord and Master of man, who himself judges and alone justifies and sanctifies – but also in which man is *God's man* – that is, the one who is accepted and received by God through his severity and goodness. Remembering the christological doctrine of the incarnation, and applying it logically, we speak of revelation as the *sublimation* of religion.

2. RELIGION AS FAITHLESSNESS

A theological evaluation of religion and the religions will certainly have to be distinguished above all by great care and compassion in making its observation and its value judgments. It will view and understand and take seriously man as the subject of religion not in separation from God, not in a human 'in-itself', but rather as the man for whom (whether he knows it or not) Jesus Christ was born, died, and was raised; as the man who (whether he has already heard or not) is intended in the Word of God; as the man who (again, whether he knows it or not) has his Lord in Christ. Religion too it will understand as a life expression and action of this man. It will thereby be prevented from attributing to this life expression and action its own 'essence' – the so-called 'essence of religion' – in order then to use this standard to weigh up and play off one human phenomenon against another, to distinguish 'higher' religion from 'lower', 'living' from 'decomposed', 'ponderable' from 'imponderable' religion. A theological evaluation will refrain from doing this – not out of carelessness or indifference towards the diversity we encounter in this human sphere as in others, nor because a provisional definition of the 'essence' of the phenomena that appear in this sphere would be impossible or inherently uninteresting. It will refrain, rather, because what we learn from God's revelation about the essence of religion does not allow us to make any but the most incidental use of an immanent definition of the essence of religion derived from elsewhere. It is not because this *revealed* essence of religion is not suited by its form and content to differentiate within human religiousness between good and evil, true and false. Not even the distinction of the church as the site of *true* religion, which is indeed given with revelation, is to be understood in such a way as to imply that the Christian religion as such were the fulfilled essence of human religion, or that the Christian religion were for that reason the true religion and fundamentally superior to the other religions. For one cannot stress too strongly the relationship of the truth of the Christian religion to the *grace* of revelation. We will have to emphasize this fact most especially: that through grace the church lives by grace and just to this extent is the site of true religion. But in that case the church will no more be able to boast of her 'essence', or the perfection in which she fulfils *the* 'essence' of religion, than she could attribute it to other religions. One will not be able, therefore, on the basis of a universal concept of the essence of religion to single out the church from the other religions and to contrast her with them.

For a truly theological examination of religion and the religions, the problem of *Nathan the Wise*[1] is therefore immaterial. Christian, Jew, and Muslim as such – and Lessing viewed them all, including the Christian, merely as such – have no advantage over one another and have nothing for which to accuse one another.

The way that Nathan/Lessing proposed that they solve the conflict – 'Let each be zealous for his uncorrupted, unprejudiced love ...' – will surely be able to lead them only deeper into their conflict, theologically considered (i.e., from the standpoint of revelation). For it is precisely from the fact that each is zealous for his love, which he will of course always take to be uncorrupted and unprejudiced, that religion and the conflict of the religions arise in the first place. Where and when have religious people not basically and generally had good intentions? In that 'eternal gospel' at the end of his *Education of the Human Race*,[2] Lessing was no doubt thinking of none other than the beginning and point of origin of all religious history. He is probably correct even theologically that the competition of the religions among themselves is an idle and artificial conflict. But he did not see that, after overcoming the artificial conflict among the various world religions including the Christian, the real religious conflict could begin at the point – which surely seems to lie beyond the possibilities of his templars or even his patriarchs – where the proclamation of God's grace over against all world religions appeared on the scene as the truth of the Christian religion. Where Christianity does that – even as one religion among others – its self-confidence is something other than religious fanaticism, its mission something other than religious propaganda; even in the form of one world religion among others, it is something other than a world religion. But it will have to be aware of itself in a most fundamental way – or better, God's grace will have to be very powerful in order to become essential for Christians *as* grace, if one is to be able to say that about Christianity.

A truly theological examination of religion and the religions, precisely as required and also possible in the church as the site of the Christian religion, will therefore have to distinguish itself from other such examinations above all by the practice of a conspicuous *patience* towards its object. Yet this patience is not to be confused with the moderation of one who, while he has his own religion or religiousness and is secretly zealous for it, nevertheless knows how to check himself, because he has told himself or been told by others that his own is not the only one, that fanaticism is just not good form, but rather that love must have the first and last word. It is not to be confused with that clever biding of one's time by the enlightened know-it-all – here is where the typical *Hegelian* philosophy of religion belongs! – who thinks he can observe, in all leisure and confident of ultimate success, the fullness of the religions in the light of a gradually evolving Idea of a perfect religion. But it is also not to be confused with the relativism and detachment of a historical scepticism that does not ask after truth and untruth in the field of religious phenomena because it thinks truth should be known only in the form of its own doubt about all truth. The inadequacy of all this alleged 'patience' shows up in the fact that the object, religion and the religions and therefore man, are not taken seriously at all but are in reality blithely ignored. Tolerance in the sense of that kind of moderation or know-it-all attitude or scepticism is in fact the worst form of intolerance. Rather, the kind of examination to be carried out on religion and the religions will

54

have to demonstrate that patience, attuned to the patience of *Christ*, which comes from the knowledge that God out of grace has reconciled godless man, together with his religion, to himself. It will see him, like an obstreperous child in its mother's arms, sustained in spite of his resistance by what God has decided and has done for his salvation. It will therefore neither praise nor blame him in particular terms, but rather it will understand his situation – not without terror before the dark enigma of this situation – but will nevertheless understand it in its enigmatical nature, not because it is meaningful in itself but rather because it acquires meaning from without, namely from Christ. But neither will it show vis-à-vis this object that falsely gentle, or superior, or weary smile of a wholly inappropriate leniency, but it will understand human beings as caught up in a way of acting that can only be recognized as right and holy to the extent that it has previously and simultaneously been recognized as utterly wrong and unholy. Needless to say, the only one willing and able to practise such patience, and therefore the theological examination of religion as well, will be the one who, along with his own religion, is prepared to bow down together with man – with every man – in the knowledge that he with his own religion first and foremost has need of patience, this powerful, supportive patience.

We begin with the proposition that religion is *faithlessness*;[3] religion is a concern – one must say, in fact, *the* concern – of *godless* man.

> 'External, gross sins are relatively insignificant when compared with the doctrine that one should become pious by means of works and by worshipping God according to our reason. For this dishonours and blasphemes the innocent blood more than anything else. The heathen committed a far greater sin by praying to the sun and the moon, which they regarded as the proper worship of God, than by sinning in any other way. Therefore the piety of man is sheer blasphemy of God and the greatest sin a man commits. Thus the ways now current in the world – the ways which the world regards as worship of God and as piety – are worse in the eyes of God than any other sin. This applies to the priests and the monks and to what seems good in the eyes of the world yet is without faith. Therefore it is better for him who does not want to obtain grace from God through the blood never to appear before the eyes of God. For by doing so he only angers the Majesty more and more'. (Luther, *Sermon on 1 Pet. 1:18 f.*, 1523)[4]

This proposition, in view of what has already been said, can have nothing to do with a negative value judgment. It contains no judgment based on religious studies or on philosophy of religion that might be grounded in some negative prejudice about the essence of religion. It is aimed not only at various others with their religion, but rather first of all at ourselves as members of the Christian religion. It formulates the judgment of divine revelation upon all religion. It can therefore be explained and expounded but can neither be derived from a higher principle than revelation nor proved with the help of a phenomenology or history of religion. Precisely because it is intended only to express the judgment of God, it signifies no human disparagement of human values, no dispute about the true, the good, and the beautiful, which upon closer examination we can discover in nearly all religions, and which we naturally expect to find in particularly abundant measure in our own religion, if we hold to it with any conviction. Where it is simply a matter of man being attacked by God, judged and condemned by God – there surely we are struck at the root, in the heart; there surely our very existence itself is called into question; but there, for just that reason, there can be no room for sad or whining laments at the failure to recognize relative human greatness.

> We do not want to neglect to add by way of warning that it also cannot be a matter of becoming a barbarian, a Christian iconoclast, in the face of human greatness as we encounter it so strikingly in this very field of religion. There was and is a certain necessity and good sense when in times of keen Christian feeling – to the distress of aesthetes everywhere – pagan temples were levelled, gods and icons of saints destroyed, stained glass smashed, organs removed. Although as irony would have it, sometimes on the very sites of these temples, and out of their very pillars and ornaments, Christian churches were soon built, and after a time the outbreak of iconoclasm was succeeded by the erection of new images in a different form. But that just goes to show that the devaluation and negation of what is human can occasionally in particular cases have practical or symbolic, but never basic or general significance. And it must not, either! We cannot, so to speak, translate the divine judgment that religion is faithlessness into human terms, into the form of specific devaluations and negations; rather, we must allow it to stand and be valid as *divine* judgment of *everything* human, even if it must be made visible from time to time in the shape of specific devaluations and negations. The only ones capable of hearing and understanding it, quite sharply and precisely as intended, will be those who have not given up completely on this human element as such, for whom rather it has some value, who have at least some inkling of what it means to abandon as such the world of the gods of Greece or India, or the world of the wisdom of China, or even the world of Roman Catholicism, or even our own Protestant world of faith – really to abandon it all in the comprehensive sense of that divine judgment. In this sense the very divine judgment that is to be heard and accepted here may also be described as a protection against all ignorance and barbarism. It calls us not to a cheap and childish resignation in the face of what is humanly great but rather to a manly knowledge of its real and ultimate limit, which does not have to be set by us but rather is already set for it. In the sphere of reverence before God, the reverence before human greatness must always have its place; it is subject to God's judgment, not ours.

In order to understand that religion is really faithlessness, we must see it from the viewpoint of the revelation attested in Holy Scripture. There are two elements that can provide the crucial clarity here.

1. Revelation is God's self-offering and self-presentation. Revelation encounters man under the presupposition and in confirmation of the fact that man's attempts to know God from his own point of view are futile – wholly and completely – on the basis not of a necessity in principle, but rather of a necessity in practice and in fact. In revelation God says to man that he is God and that as such he is his, man's, Lord. Revelation thereby tells him something utterly new, something that without revelation he does not know and cannot tell himself or others. It is true, of course, that he *could* do it, since it is certain that revelation expresses only the truth. If it is true that God is God and as such is man's Lord, then it is also true that man is in such a relationship to him that he could know him. But this very truth is not available to man until it is told to him in revelation. If he is really *able* to know God, then this ability is based on the fact that he actually knows him because God has given himself to him to be known, because God has offered and presented himself to him. This ability is thus based not on the fact – true though it is – that man could actually know him. Between 'he could' and 'he can' lies 'he cannot', which utterly separates them, and which by revelation, and only by revelation, is sublimated[5] and turned into its opposite. The truth that God is God and our Lord, and thus that we could also know him as God and Lord – this truth can come to us only through the truth itself. This coming-to-us of truth *is* revelation. But revelation does not reach us in a neutral state but rather in an act that stands in a quite definite, indeed a determined, relationship to it as the coming-to-us of truth. It reaches us, namely, as *religious* people, that is, it reaches us in the midst of that attempt to know God from our own point of view. It does not reach us, therefore, in an act that corresponds to itself. The act that corresponds to revelation would, after all, have to be faith: the acknowledgment of God's self-offering and self-presentation. We would have to see that in relation to God our every act is in vain, even in the best life – that is, that we are not in a position to grasp the truth by ourselves, to let God be God and our Lord. We would therefore really have to refrain from all attempts to grasp this truth. We would have to be ready and resolved once and for all to let the truth speak to us and thus to be grasped by it. But for that we are precisely not ready and resolved. The very man to whom the truth has actually come will admit that he was by no means ready and resolved to let it speak to him. The very man of faith will not say that he has come to faith out of faith but precisely out of faithlessness – even though the attitude and act with which he approached, and still approaches, revelation is religion. Precisely the religion of man as such, however, is exposed by revelation, by faith in revelation, as *resistance* to it. Religion, seen from the viewpoint of revelation, becomes visible as the enterprise by which man anticipates that which God wills to do and does do in his revelation, putting a human contraption in place of the divine handiwork. In other words, in place of the divine reality that offers and

presents itself to us in revelation, religion puts an image of God that man has wilfully and arbitrarily devised for himself.

> 'Man's perpetual genius, so to speak, is to be a factory of idols ... Man is tempted to express outwardly in works the God he has inwardly conceived. Therefore the mind begets an idol; the hand gives it birth' (Calvin).[6]

Here 'wilfully and arbitrarily' just means for the moment 'out of his own means, his own insight and will-power and energy'. The images of God that can be constructed, once one has embarked on this enterprise, can vary greatly from one another without their actually meaning something different.

> 'But God does not compare these images with one another, as if one were more suitable, another less so; but without exception he repudiates all likenesses, pictures, and other signs by which the superstitious have thought he will be near them' (Calvin).[7] '[He] returns to nothingness whatever divinity men fashion for themselves out of their own opinion' (ibid.).[8] The ultimate principles of the various philosophical systems are just as much images of God in the sense of this enterprise as, for example, the essence of the uncanny in the world view of the animistic religions; the highly developed idea of God in Islam, for example, just as much as the lack of a unified concept and image of God in Buddhism or in the atheistic spiritual movements of the ancient and modern worlds.

The image of God is always that reality, seen or thought, in which man assumes and asserts something Real, Ultimate, Decisive beyond or even within his own existence, by which he in turn takes himself to be posited or at least determined and conditioned. Seen from the viewpoint of revelation, human religion is, after a fashion, such an assumption and assertion and as such it is an act that contradicts revelation. It contradicts it because the truth can come to man only through the truth. If man grasps at the truth on his own, then of necessity it eludes his grasp. So he does not do what he would have to do when the truth comes to him. So, then, he does not have faith. If he had faith he would *listen*; but in religion he *talks*. If he had faith he would allow something to be *given* to him; but in religion he *takes* something for himself. If he had faith he would let God himself stand up for God; but in religion he dares that grasping after God. Because it is this *grasping*, religion is the contradiction to revelation, the concentrated expression of the human lack of faith, that is, the attitude and activity directly opposed to faith. It is the feeble but also defiant, the high-spirited but also helpless attempt – by means of something that man could indeed do but now cannot do – to create the very thing that he can only create because and if God himself creates it for him: knowledge of the truth, knowledge of God. So this attempt cannot be interpreted, for instance, as though man by doing it were cooperating harmoniously with God's revelation, as though religion were the outstretched hand that God would then fill in his revelation. Neither can one say of the manifest religious capacity of man that it is, so to speak, the universal form of human knowledge, which then receives its true and proper content in the shape of revelation and faith. Here, rather, it is a matter of utter contradiction: in religion man resists and closes himself off to revelation by creating a substitute for it, by anticipating something that should be given him in revelation by God.

> 'They do not therefore apprehend God as he offers himself, but imagine him as they have fashioned him in their own presumption' (Calvin).[9]

He does indeed have the capability for such an act. But what he gains and achieves on the basis of this capability is never the knowledge of God as God and Lord, and thus never the truth but rather a complete and utter fiction, which has not just a little but nothing to do with God. This anti-God must first be recognized as such and then fall when the truth comes to him, but it can only be recognized as such and as fiction *by* the truth coming to him.

> 'For such knowledge of God as now remains in men is nothing else than a frightful source of idolatry and of all superstitions' (Calvin, commentary on John 3:6).[10]

Revelation does not hook up with the already present and operative religion of man but rather contradicts it, just as religion previously contradicted revelation; revelation sublimates religion, just as religion previously sublimated revelation.[11] In the same way, faith cannot hook up with false faith but must contradict it – sublimate it – as faithlessness, as an act of contradiction.

> The rejection of gentile religion in the Old Testament is directed with surprising one-sidedness against its *worship of images*. Image worship as such, on behalf of whatever god, is objectionable. In support of this judgment it is maintained again and again – in detail, e.g., in Jer. 10:1–16 and Isa. 44:9–20 – that in the pagan religions man himself was originally the creator of his god. I think it is unlikely that such passages can be explained by saying that the biblical authors did not know, or out of crass prejudice did not want to know, what the Catholic Church has always said in explanation and defence of its customary veneration of images, and what is today a virtual commonplace in religious studies – that the divine image is never originally and properly regarded as identical with the divinity in question, but rather that the divinity is worshipped and adored in the divine image only as in its placeholder and representative, while the image as such is offered only a figuratively intended *douleia* [veneration]. I think it is much more likely that the reproach of 'idol-making' (Isa. 44:9; 45:16) is aimed, in full knowledge of this situation, at spiritual idol-making, the index of which

59

is the fabrication of images. For those 'other' gods, the 'foreign' gods whom the people Israel is repeatedly forbidden to 'cleave unto' or to 'fall prey to', as though to sin itself – they are not called 'other' simply because they are the gods of other peoples, as though Yahweh were zealous against them only for the sake of his honour, just because he is the God of the people Israel. Rather, they are 'other' and 'foreign' first of all to Yahweh himself: they in their way to him in his way. And the reason is because of the fact that they can even have such placeholders and representatives in the images of gods made by human hands, while he, Yahweh, can be modelled by no human work, because his name is holy, because he himself wills in *his* work to witness exclusively to himself, to be his own mediator – in his revelation, in his action as Lord of the covenant, in his commandments, in his word entrusted to the prophets. Behind the worship of those other gods, as shown by its character as image worship, stands man's wilfulness and arbitrariness. Therefore Israel must not succumb to them. And the urgency of this ban, and of image worship generally, even when it is applied to Yahweh, must be understood in relation to the fact that Yahweh, as the God of the divine self-revelation that stands in opposition to man's wilfulness and arbitrariness, wills to be acknowledged and honoured. It should be noted that the same thing that among the gentiles at first appears only to be *foolishness*, becomes concretely visible in the realm of Israel, hence in the realm of revelation and the covenant, as *sin*. Measured by revelation, what the gentiles are attempting with regard to God is the sin of *faithlessness*. Because Israel has been made a participant in the divine self-revelation, it may neither take part in the image worship of the gentile religions, nor even make and venerate images of Yahweh. It would at once betray Yahweh radically with the latter no less than with the former.

The remarkable New Testament expansion of this observation we find in the passages Rom. 1:18f. and Acts 14:15f.; 17:22f. (The passage Rom. 2:14f. does not come into consideration here: the gentiles in whom the prophecy of Jer. 31:33 has been fulfilled are, according to whole context of the chapter, to be understood unambiguously as gentile *Christians*.) The revelation of righteousness, i.e., of the will of God in Jesus Christ that creates and grants righteousness on earth out of grace – this fulfilment of all revelation has now made distinguishing between the gentiles and Israel into a matter of secondary importance. Israel's Messiah, having appeared and been rejected and crucified by Israel itself, has revealed himself as Lord of the whole world. But this does not only mean that there is a grace of God for all human beings of all nations. It also means that all are now drawn into responsibility and accountability in the same way that previously applied only to Israel. So it does not only mean that the *covenant* made between God and man is now to be proclaimed to *all* peoples as the good news that applies to them as well. It also means that the charge of *apostasy* is now to be raised expressly and seriously against them *all*. To speak in the words of Acts 14:16: the times are now over when 'God in past generations allowed all the nations to walk in their own ways.' And in the words of Acts 17:30: 'The times of ignorance God overlooked, but now (in and with the Now that has entered in Jesus Christ) he commands all men everywhere to repent.' For the saving revelation of God's righteousness is also at the same time the revelation of God's wrath against the ungodliness and wickedness (*asebeia kai adikia*) of humans (Rom. 1:18); where *forgiveness* of sins becomes manifest, there too sins are uncovered, condemned, and punished as such. What does this mean? Not, namely, according to Rom. 1 as well as Acts 14 and 17, what one might at first understand by 'ungodliness' and 'wickedness' – not a profane, secular attitude turned away from the divine, but rather the worship that man offers in goodwill to that which he takes to be divine. This goodwill and the truth of the divinity of this 'divinity' is flatly denied him by God's revelation in Christ, and by his confrontation with this revelation. The supposedly best that human beings do, namely this divine worship of theirs, is precisely 'ungodliness' and 'wickedness'. Their piety is 'fear of demons' (Acts 17:22).[12] They worship beings that by their nature are not gods at all (Gal. 4:8). They are therefore, in and with their piety, ones 'without God in the world' (Eph. 2:12). And from the point of view of the revelation made and fulfilled in Christ, one must from now on say of all people what previously, by the revelation in the Old Testament prophecy, was to be said only of unfaithful Israel: precisely in the best that they have done, they have acted sinfully towards God. In just this way they have 'suppressed the truth in wickedness' (Rom. 1:18). Christ having appeared, died, and been raised, so that the grace of God has become an event for all people, all people are now made responsible for what they are and what they do – specifically, for what they are and do as it appears in light of this event. This means, however, because this event is the self-revelation of the truth and therefore also of the truth about man, it is the deepest and ultimate human reality. Seen from the perspective of the self-revelation of truth, what we are and do as humans is, in its deepest and ultimate reality, in conflict with the truth. It is *opposed* to the truth as it reveals itself there by an angle of 180 degrees. In and with the proclamation of Christ (it is to be noted that this is the presupposition of Rom. 1 as well as those speeches in Acts) one must say outright to human beings, to whom this proclamation is directed and who are instructed by it about the relationship of God and man, i.e. about God's grace – one must say to them that in their opposition they occupy a relationship to the truth, which they deny and betray *through* that opposition. Because God's grace is proclaimed in Christ, they must concede: God 'did not leave himself without witness' (Acts 14:17). For precisely in and with the proclamation of God's grace in Christ, God's witness is disclosed to them, which they have forsaken and to which they have come into radical opposition. By entering into the light of this proclamation, this witness awakens and arises, it speaks, becomes a witness against them, so that they stand there as unexcused and inexcusable before the God who encounters them in his revelation (Rom. 1:20).

In the speeches of the Acts of the Apostles this witness – disclosed, awakening, and accusing – spoken to all people in and with the proclamation of Christ, is their knowledge of God as *creator*. 'He did good and gave you from heaven rains and fruitful seasons, satisfying your hearts with food and gladness' (Acts 14:17). He is the one! They come to know this anew. And they also now come to know completely anew – that they already knew it! Have they not confirmed it by erecting, in 'unknowing piety' (*agnoountes eusebeite*, Acts 17:23), an altar to the 'unknown God'? By proclaiming God in Christ to them, Paul is saying to them: you knew about this very God, this very God has in you been turned from a known into an unknown God, because you have worshipped him in unknowing piety. Before this very God, therefore, whom I now make known to you again, you stand as the accused who are unable to excuse themselves. This God – I *say* this to you now out of my knowledge of Christ, I *assign* this to you now as your own knowledge in and in spite of your complete ignorance: this God created the world and everything that is in it; he is the Lord of heaven and earth; he made man and guides human history. Therefore, because it is so, because human beings belong to this God, it can now happen that they seek God, whether they would grasp and find him, even though he – O human folly! – is not far from each one of us, even though in him we live and move and have our being and therefore do not need first to seek him, even though the unknowing knowledge of one of your poets himself testifies, 'We are of his race', and therefore: He is near to us, as a father is near to his children. If this is true (and it is true!), if we know this (and we do know it!), then why that seeking, that grasping and wanting to find God, in which I see you caught up? Because God is the creator and therefore the Lord – and in Christ it has become obvious for time and eternity that it is so – therefore, and only therefore, are we *able* to sin in idolatry. But why do we *do* this? Because we must acknowledge that God is the creator and therefore the Lord, just as it has been told us – and in Christ it has been told us as something well known, something already told us – for this reason we must recognize our idolatry as sin, as 'ungodliness' and 'wickedness' – so why don't we do it? How can the Lord of heaven and earth dwell in a temple made by hands, be served by human hands – he, from whom we have life and breath and everything? How can we, who are his offspring and children and who therefore already belong to him, worship the divinity in an object made of gold, silver, or stone; an object of our seeking, grasping, and finding, brought about by human art and ingenuity; in the form of one of our own attempted approximations? If God is the creator, how can there be such a thing as a mediation that we ourselves establish? How utterly impossible is all of this! And yet so real: this struggle against the grace of revelation in favour of a wilful and arbitrary attempt to storm heaven! In this struggle against grace the known God has become an unknown one. There is no future for opposition to the truth once the truth has pressed itself upon us as such in God's revelation (Acts 17:24–9). There remains really nothing else for us to do – really nothing for *us* to do – but to 'turn from these vain things to the living God' (Acts 14:15).

We encounter the same line of thought, though with a characteristically different emphasis, in the Letter to the Romans. That witness which the apostle addresses to the gentiles in and with the proclamation of Christ, thus awakening it in them and asserting it against them, is here highlighted as their knowledge of *God* the Creator. Precisely the invisible, unapproachable nature of God, his eternal power and divinity, has been grasped and seen in his works (Rom. 1:20). People always start precisely from an acquaintance with God, in fact from an acquaintance on the basis of revelation, because revelation comes to them in Christ (Rom. 1:19). And therefore it is really a suppressing of the truth, a 'corruption of the best', of which they can be accused (Rom. 1:18). One should bear in mind that even these words, which have so often been understood as a permission or invitation to every possible kind of natural theology, are in reality a component of the apostolic kerygma, whatever the contemporary philosophical notions to which they may seem to allude. In order to make clear what is involved in the revelation of the righteousness of God in Christ (Rom. 1:17; 3:21), Paul reminds us in Rom. 1:18 to 3:20 that the very *same* one revelation is also a revelation of God's *wrath*, that is, that when we are told of the grace that has come to us we must also see and believe our utter liability to judgment. Grace as well as judgment apply to gentile as well as Jew, to Jew as well as gentile (Rom. 1:16; 2:9), and in fact to Jew and gentile at their best, in their worship of God. It is a Christian statement, one presupposing revelation, when Paul says with regard to the Jews that the knowledge of sin comes through the law (Rom. 3:20). So likewise it is under the presupposition of the event that has taken place between God and man in Christ, that it is said that the knowledge of God from the works of creation found among the gentiles is the instrument for making them inexcusable and therefore for submitting them, along with the Jews, to the judgment and thus to the grace of God. It is also no different here: because *Christ* was born, died, and rose again, there is no longer any abstract, self-contained, stable gentile world. And because Paul has this Christ to proclaim, *therefore* he can appeal to the gentiles on the grounds that they too belong fully to God and know about God, that God is in fact revealed to them too, has made himself known to them in the works of creation as God – his eternal power and divinity, which is none other than that of Jesus Christ. *Therefore* he can say to them that through this knowledge of theirs they are without excuse before God when they 'suppress' the truth through their ungodliness and wickedness. One cannot understand what Paul says about the gentiles in Rom. 1:19–20 apart from the situation of the apostolic preaching, apart from the Word's becoming flesh, and therefore most definitely not as an abstract proposition about the gentiles themselves, about a revelation possessed by the gentiles as their own. Paul knows neither Jews nor gentiles in themselves and as such, but rather he knows only the Jews and gentiles placed under the promise by the cross of Christ but placed also under the commandment of God. Because the prophetic revelation in Christ fulfils the witness of Israel's expectation; because Israel, by crucifying its Messiah, founders on that revelation; because it has now become revelation to both Jews and gentiles; because it now concerns the gentiles too – for all these reasons, the gentiles come to stand under the claim and demand of revelation just as emphatically as the Jews. Like the Jews, they need to be told that man – not by himself but by virtue of God's revelation – knows God very well and therefore knows that he stands guilty before him, knows this from the creation ('since the creation of the world', Rom. 1:20, i.e. in and with their own existence and that of the whole world). The status of the gentiles like the status of the Jews is objectively different after the death and resurrection of Christ than before. From the perspective of Christ, the gentiles too are now placed along with the Jews under the heavens that are telling the glory of God and upon the firmament that proclaims his handiwork (Ps. 19:2); the gentiles too are to be addressed as 'ones who know God' (Rom. 1:21) – but with the immediate reservation that they, like the Jews, have *not* shown themselves to be such ('did not see fit to acknowledge God', Rom. 1:28). It is not, therefore, as though Paul were somehow in a position to appeal to a knowledge, possessed by the gentiles, of the invisible nature of God as revealed to them from creation. He could not begin pedagogically with this knowledge, nor could he in proclaiming Jesus Christ create the impression even for a moment that he was talking about things already known to them on the basis of that 'original revelation'. For the gentiles have never realized the knowledge of Ps. 19 in principle even in the slightest way. They have not in fact shown God honour and thanks as God (Rom. 1:21). That means, as the continuation shows, not merely a quantitative failure in their service towards him nor an imperfection in their relationship to him. It means, rather, that the *doxazein kai eucharistein* [honour and thanks] that they owe to God never takes place at all, that another meditation, thought, and action has taken its place, one that (in *negation* of the idea that God is revealed to man from creation) at its root just does not have God as its object. 'They became futile in their thinking and their senseless minds were darkened' (Rom. 1:21). 'Claiming (to themselves and others) to be wise, they became fools' (Rom. 1:22). And the result was sheer catastrophe: 'they exchanged the glory of the immortal God for images resembling mortal man or birds or animals or reptiles' (Rom. 1:23) – with these images 'they exchanged the truth about God for a lie and worshipped and served the creature rather than the Creator, who is blessed for ever! Amen' (Rom. 1:25) – an exchange that then inevitably proved to be horrifying in the obvious moral confusion of the human race. Paul says not one word to suggest that the gentiles in spite of this apostasy had preserved a remnant of 'natural' knowledge of God. On the contrary, he states without reservation: against this apostasy the wrath of God has now been revealed; 'those who do such things deserve to die' (Rom. 1:32). Revelation, which had again and again contradicted the gentile religion within the sphere of the people of Israel on the soil of Palestine, now that Jesus Christ has died for all also contradicts it 'publicly', also in its own gentile sphere, in an apostolic letter directed in remarkable fashion precisely to the Christians in Rome. There is now no longer any unchallenged gentile world, one that is relatively possible, one that remains excusable. When revelation comes on the scene, when its light falls upon the gentile world, then its religion is examined and exposed as the opposite of revelation, as the false religion of faithlessness.

2. Revelation, as God's self-offering and self-presentation, is the act by which, out of grace and by means of grace, he reconciles man with himself. As a radical teaching about God, it is at the same time God's radical help, which comes to us as those who are unrighteous and unholy, and as such damned and lost. In this respect as well, the conclusion established and presupposed by revelation in relation to man is that man cannot help himself – neither wholly, nor even just in part. In this respect as well, it is the case, to be sure, that man is not helpless by necessity. It is not, after all, inherent in the concept of man to be unrighteous and unholy and thus damned and lost. For he is really made in the image of God, that is, for obedience to God and not for sin, for his salvation and not for his perdition. But here, too, he is to be approached not as one in a state in which he somehow still finds himself, but rather as one in a state in which he no longer finds himself, and from which he has fallen through his own fault. This truth he is also unable to prove; it is not available to him unless it comes to him in revelation, that is, in Jesus Christ, to be declared to him anew – this oldest

truth wholly new! He cannot in any sense declare to himself that he is just and holy, and thus saved; because in his own mouth as his own judgment of himself it would be a lie. It is truth as God's revealed knowledge. It is truth in Jesus Christ. Jesus Christ does not somehow augment and improve all the human attempts to conceive and present God by human standards; rather, as God's self-offering and self-presentation, he replaces them, thereby simply surpassing them and putting them in the shadows where they belong. In this way, since in him God reconciles the world with himself, he also replaces all human attempts to reconcile God with the world, all human attempts at justification and sanctification, at conversion and salvation. God's revelation in Jesus Christ means that our justification and our sanctification, our conversion and our salvation, has taken place and been consummated once and for all in Jesus Christ. And our faith in Jesus Christ consists in our acknowledging, approving, affirming, and accepting that everything has happened for us too once and for all in Jesus Christ. He is the help that comes to us, he alone the Word of God himself, spoken to us, the exchange of status between him and us: his righteousness and holiness are ours; our sin is his; he for us is a lost one, we for his sake are the saved. With this exchange (*katallage*, 2 Cor. 5:19) revelation stands or falls. It would not be God's effective, salutary self-offering and self-presentation if it were not centrally and decisively this: the satisfaction and intercession of Jesus Christ.

And now the second way is evident in which revelation contradicts religion and in which conversely religion must contradict revelation. Why, then, in all religions this endeavour to anticipate God, to foist a human contrivance in the place of his word, to make our own images – first spiritual, then intellectual, and finally even visual – of the one who is known only where he gives himself to be known? What, then, does religious man want by thinking, believing, and maintaining the existence of that unique, ultimate, and decisive being; the existence of a divinity (*theion*), a godhead; the existence of gods, and even a single supreme god – and by taking himself to be posited, determined, conditioned, and ruled by it? Is the postulate of the god or gods and the need to objectify them intellectually in sensuous form the primary thing, conditioned by the human experience of the actual superiority and power of certain natural and supernatural, historical and timeless, necessities, potencies, and structures? Does this experience (or the corresponding postulate and need) *precede* the feeling of human impotence and transgression in the face of this higher world, the urge to put oneself in a peaceful and friendly relation with it, to interest it in human beings, to ensure its support, or better still, to gain influence over it, to participate in its power and dignity, to cooperate in its work? Does man's attempt to justify and sanctify himself *follow* the attempt at the idea of God and the image of God? Or is the relationship precisely the opposite? Is the primary thing man's obscure urge to justify and sanctify himself, i.e., to confirm and strengthen himself in the awareness and exercise of his skill and power at mastering life, at coming to terms with the world, at making the world serve his needs? Is religion with its dogmatics and worship and rules for life the most primitive – or better perhaps, the most intimate and intensive – component of the technique by means of which man tries to cope with his existence? Is perhaps the experience of that higher world, or the need to objectify it in the idea or image of God, to be understood simply as an exponent of this attempt, namely, as the unavoidable ideal construction within the framework of that technique? Are the gods only the reflected images and guarantees of the needs and capacities of man, who in reality is alone, dependent on himself and his own willing, ordering, and making? Might sacrifice, prayer, asceticism, and morality in religion be more primitive than God and the gods? Who is to say? In the face of these two possibilities we surely find ourselves in a circle that can be looked at and understood one way or the other with the same result. What is certain is that religion, also from this side, also with regard to its practical content, has to do with an attitude and activity corresponding not to God's revelation but rather to its opposite. Here again weakness and defiance, helplessness and arrogance, folly and fantasy, are so close to one another that one can scarcely be distinguished from the other. Where man wants what he wants in religion, justification and sanctification as his own work, there he finds himself – regardless of whether the idea and image of God are of primary or only secondary importance to the project – not on the way to God, who could then still bring him to the goal via some higher stage of the same way. Rather, he is about to close himself off from God, to alienate himself from him, even to come into direct opposition to him. For God in his revelation does not will that man attempt to cope with his existence by himself, to justify and sanctify himself. God in his revelation, God in Jesus Christ, is precisely the one who takes away the sin of the world, who wills that all our care be cast upon him, because he cares for us.

'... by this article our faith is separated from all other faiths on earth. For the Jews have it not, neither do the Turks and Saracens, nor any Papist or false Christian or any other unbeliever, but only proper Christians. So when you come to Turkey, where you can have neither preachers nor books, there say to yourself, be it in bed or at work, be it in words or thoughts, your 'Our Father', the Creed, and the Ten Commandments; and when you come to this article, cross your fingers or make some sort of sign with your hand or foot, so that you may imagine this article and make note of it, and especially, for example, where you see some Turkish stumbling-block or are tempted. And with your 'Our Father', pray that God may keep you from stumbling and hold you pure and steadfast in this article, for in the article lies your life and blessedness' (Luther, Military Sermon against the Turks, 1529).[13]

The characteristically pious element of the pious effort to reconcile him to ourselves is the very thing that must be an abomination to God, whether idolatry is judged to be its presupposition or its consequence, or perhaps both. Not by somehow continuing along this line but only by breaking off and ending it can man reach, not his own goal, but God's goal, which stands directly opposed to his own.

'Therefore I have often said that to speak and judge rightly in this matter we must carefully distinguish between a pious man (what philosophers call a *bonum virum* [good man]) and a Christian. We too approve of being a pious man, and indeed there is nothing more praiseworthy on earth, and it is God's gift, just as much as sun and moon, grain and wine, and all creation. But let us not mix and brew them together, but rather let a pious man have his praise before the world and say: A pious man is indeed a splendid and precious man on earth, but is not therefore a Christian. For he may be a Turk or a pagan (as in ancient times some have been highly praised). Indeed it cannot be otherwise, than that among so many bad men a good man must at times be found. But however pious he may be, he is and remains for all such piety Adam's child, that is, an earthly man, under sin and death.

'But if you ask about a Christian, you must go much higher. For this is a different man, one who is not called Adam's child and has no father and mother on earth, but is God's child, an heir and nobleman in the kingdom of heaven. But he is called a Christian for this reason: that with his heart he depends on this Saviour, who has ascended to the Father, and believes that for his sake and by him he has God's grace and eternal redemption and life. That is neither achieved nor grasped, obtained nor learned by our own life, virtue, and work, by which we are called pious people on earth, neither by righteousness according to the Law and Ten Commandments, which is nevertheless necessary, as was said, and is also found in every Christian. But this chief thing and righteousness is still far from achieved, of which Christ here speaks and which he calls righteousness' (Luther, *Sermon on John 16:5–15*, 1545).[14]

It is a mistake – one not to be justified by its venerable age, and which even Luther played a part in reinforcing – whenever one understands the *Old Testament* as a document, possibly the classical document, of a religion of law and thus of works, and therefore, since all religion as such is a religion of works, as a document of religion in general. The Israel that understands the 'Do this, and you will live' (Luke 10:28) to mean that man has to justify and sanctify himself by fulfilling the law in his own works is not the true Israel. Here, rather, one wants to be under the law without wanting to hear the law (Gal. 4:21). Here, rather, sin has become 'sinful beyond measure' (*kath' huperbolen hamartolos*, Rom. 7:13), by making use of the law (Rom. 7:8, 11), by committing the greatest deceit by means of the law (Rom. 7:11). In view of the law, with its 'Thou shalt not covet', it causes 'desire' (*epithumia*) to spring up in us (Rom. 7:7). In what does this 'desire' consist, and hence the sin that dwells within us (Rom. 7:17)? It apparently consisted, already according to the story of the fall into sin of the first human being (Gen. 3:1f.), not primarily in the desire for the fruit of that tree as such but rather in the spiritual, or pseudo-spiritual, desire through the consumption of this fruit to become like God and to know what is good and evil. It is this 'desire' which, through the deception that sin commits with the law, acquires in Israel new – and here indeed for the first time – real power (Gal. 3:19, Rom. 5:20, 1 Cor. 15:56). 'They have a zeal for God, but it is not enlightened. For, being ignorant of the righteousness that comes from God, and seeking to establish their own, they did not submit to God's righteousness' (Rom. 10:2–3). To the lawyer's question, 'What shall I do to inherit eternal life?' Jesus answers with the simple reference to the law. But how does the man take this suggestion? 'But he, desiring to justify himself ...' (Lk. 10:25–29; cf. 16:15). That is the 'desire' of the one whom sin has deceived by means of the law! It is never the true Israel that has succumbed to this desire, and it is never the meaning of the Old Testament that is realized in this desire. Here instead strives that Israel over whose minds a veil lies to this day whenever Moses is read (2 Cor. 3:15). Here strives that Israel which, pursuing a 'righteousness which is based on law', did not succeed in fulfilling that law (Rom. 9:31). Here Israel is wrecked upon the rock on which it is founded because it will not believe (Rom. 9:32–33). The law given it by God is in truth *spiritual* (Rom. 7:14). It is not against the promises (Gal. 3:21). *Christ* is the end of the law: that everyone who has faith may be justified (Rom. 10:4). Here, by that Israel that crucifies its Messiah, the law is not kept but 'weakened' (Rom. 8:3) and broken in pieces (Rom. 2:17f.). And therefore the law is directed here as from time immemorial *against* Israel (Rom. 2:12; 3:19). It brings wrath (Rom. 4:15). It kills (2 Cor. 3:6; Rom. 7:5, 13). The same curse that once came upon the fathers because of their disobedience to Moses, because of their persecution of the prophets, because of their fornication with the Baalim – the same curse comes upon Pharisaic Israel whose lawfulness is the same sin in another form as its old lawlessness. 'You who boast in the law, do you dishonour God by breaking the law?' (Rom. 2:23). 'All day long I have held out my hands to a disobedient and contrary people' (Rom. 10:21). The new works-righteousness is at root none other than the old idolatry. And the old idolatry was already at root none other than works-righteousness. To understand this equation one might read Stephen's speech in Acts 7:2-53 with its devastating final judgment: '... you who received the law as delivered by angels and did not keep it'. The way of the true Israel, of the people that the Lord made the people of his covenant though his Word, therefore truly cannot have been the way from idolatry to works-righteousness. The true Israel, that is, Isaiah's remnant (Rom. 9:29), the seven thousand in Israel who have not bowed the knee to Baal (Rom. 11:4) – they were obedient to God's law by keeping in and with his *first* commandment all the others, but that means they received and accepted grace as grace, lived by the Word of God, waited on God, looked to the hands of God as the eyes of a servant look to the hands of his master (Ps. 123:2). The true Israel therefore could not deviate from the law, and also therefore could not want to justify and sanctify itself by misusing the law, because the law as 'law of the Spirit of life' (Rom. 8:2) had been given to it in its heart and written upon its mind (Jer. 31:33; Rom. 2:28f.), and for this reason, so that its iniquity would be forgiven and its sin remembered no more (Jer. 31:34; Rom. 4:6). As such a gift and inscription, the law was for Israel the direct power of God, which necessarily protected it, the justified and sanctified Israel, from deviation to the left *or* to the right. Precisely the witness of this Israel and thus the witness of the coming Jesus Christ is the meaning of the Old Testament, and it is therefore not the document of a religion of works but rather, together with the New Testament, the document of the revelation that contradicts every religion of works and thereby religion itself.

Luther's position on this matter cannot be reduced to one common denominator. As an interpreter of the Old and New Testaments, he often distinguished in an excessively abstract and schematic way between law and gospel, between commandments and promises, and even between Old and New Testaments as a whole, in a Paulinism that was not that of Paul himself. But then he would again perceive and understand with surprising clarity the original and ultimate unity of the two.[15] We will focus on this *second* Luther. Already in 1522 and without alteration at the end of his life, in the conclusion of his Preface to the Letter to the Romans (1546), he reduced the content of this apostolic writing to the following remarkable formula: 'Therefore it appears that [St Paul] wanted in this one epistle to sum up briefly the whole Christian and evangelical doctrine, and to prepare an introduction to the entire Old Testament. For, without doubt, whoever has this epistle well in his heart, has with him the light and power of the Old Testament. Therefore let every Christian be familiar with it and exercise himself in it continually. To this end may God give his grace. Amen.'[16] If one has, precisely in Romans, the light and power of the Old Testament with one, then it is hard to see why the light and power of precisely the Old Testament and its holy, just, and good law should not also be seen as *grace*, and its opposition to justification and sanctification by works seen as opposition to *the* human sin.

With regard to the New Testament, must one not draw special attention to the fact that it, like the Old Testament, is law – i.e., ordinance, command, and instruction for the new life of the people and the children of God – but not therefore – not even in part – an authorization and invitation to self-justification and self-sanctification? It is therefore not a book of religion but rather the consistent proclamation of the justifying and sanctifying grace of God, thereby exposing the faithlessness in all religion. One must, however, expressly draw attention to this fact again and again, because the simple insight that the New Testament is witness to Jesus Christ and nothing else can never lie behind us as an insight already accomplished but needs to be newly accomplished again and again in the struggle with the error of our ears and our heart. For one is in the habit of repeatedly overlooking the fact that the *form* also of the New Testament witness is not only, for example, in the Sermon on the Mount, in the letter of James, in the paranetic[17] chapters of Paul, but is all along, strictly speaking, the *law*. One forgets, then, what is so clear and self-evident, that the essence of the benefit of Jesus Christ and therefore of his gospel as experienced in the church of the New Testament is his *Lordship* over human beings. And there can be no purer, or more total *imperative* than the simple invitation directed to man in the New Testament – that he should believe in this Jesus Christ – and no stricter or fuller *obedience* than that which the New Testament describes precisely as faith. Here not the least has been lost from that energy with which man in the Old Testament is claimed for Yahweh alone, and wholly for Yahweh. But precisely if one overlooks this fact and splits up the New Testament texts too into words of gospel, promise, comfort, on the one hand, and of law, ethics, imperatives, on the other; precisely if one does not understand them as law also in their entirety; precisely if in the preaching of the Johannine Baptist about the Lamb of God who takes away the sins of the world one no longer hears directly the preaching of repentance that is attributed to him in the synoptic gospels – precisely if one thinks in this way, then the second error all too easily creeps in, where it seems as if there were in the New Testament, *alongside* the gospel, that is, *alongside* the message of the reconciliation of the world with God that has taken place in Christ, some other such thing as a new law, as though the gospel in the New Testament acquired a moral character only afterwards, since it appeals not only to faith but in addition to something else entirely, namely, to the free decision of the human will, since it calls on man to make good his justification and sanctification that happened in Christ in certain attitudes and actions – as though the word about reconciliation only became a serious matter in light of this second word about the new life. In this case the viewpoint we have to adopt in hearing the New Testament message must constantly change: at one time we have to think of Christ and his work, at another of the improvement of our own position; at one time we have to place everything in God's hands, but at another to take everything into our own hands again; at one time we have to believe and at another to love and to do all kinds of good. And there follows almost unavoidably upon this second error the third, the reversal of the relationship between the two components of the New Testament message that are abstracted and characterized in this way. Doubtless the second group of New Testament utterances, misunderstood as new law, is disproportionately much easier to understand, more plausible and manageable than the first, of which it is agreed that it speaks abstractly of grace from above, of Jesus Christ and his work, of the forgiveness of sins, of the gift of the Holy Spirit. Who would want to waste much time and attention on a matter that is so obscure, lofty, and easy to misunderstand as intellectualistic? What we would like to see are actions. Life urges on us its questions and tasks and above all the opportunities that man always thinks he has in relation to them. It is precisely to these opportunities that the new law we think we have discovered in the New Testament seems to direct us. When we appreciate the New Testament from this perspective, we are basically once again on our own, in the familiar sphere of our abilities, ventures, projects, accomplishments. The whole mystery of the New Testament, together with the oppressive but also joyful responsibility that it signifies, becomes our own mystery. Why should we not appreciate it first and foremost from this perspective, saving the other perspective for special occasions, for periodic efforts, should they be needed, at recommitment to our own ethical fulfilment! Is it as indispensable to us as we continually affirm? Do we really still have any use for it? Doesn't it bother us just a little bit that the New Testament nevertheless seems to have this other perspective as well? Be that as it may, our attention, our love, our emphasis, our enthusiasm is no longer there but here, with the much more practical matter of our self-justification and self-sanctification, against the background of our assurance that of course the work of Christ and the gift of the Holy Spirit are the decisive starting point for us. In these three stages we see the process taking place, which again and again suggests itself to every reader of the New Testament, of re-translating its message back into the document of a religion.

And so our concern must be again and again to make this process impossible at its very root – namely, at the point where the New Testament tends to break apart in the two different groups of (a) passivities, and (b) motivations. This distinction amounts to nothing! It may even be better to start by understanding the New Testament wholly as law alone rather than by understanding it in this distinction between law and gospel! For it is surely true that faith in the New Testament message is man's justification *and* sanctification, his new position before God *and* his new life here and now. It is both, however, because it is wholly and solely faith in *Jesus Christ*. As such perhaps faith is quite rightly understood first of all wholly as *obedience* to the *Lord* Jesus Christ, and the New Testament message therefore wholly as *law*. There is much to be said for understanding sanctification – i.e., the fact that man is claimed by God, that he belongs to God by grace (in the sense developed by Calvin in the third book of the *Institutes*) – as the higher, or at least the formally prior, reality within faith. But however one may order the concepts, in the New Testament faith is under all circumstances faith in Jesus Christ. One may understand faith more as trust or more as obedience, or first as trust and then as obedience, or the other way around – but one thing is certain: that one can understand it only from its object, from Jesus Christ; but that means in opposition to the claim of the believer's own work. Since the believer in the New Testament sense, together with all his activity and work, is claimed by Jesus Christ, belongs to him, this claim of his own activity and work is struck down decisively, and not only is the expectation of being able to help himself taken from him, but also the permission to want to do so. Faith in the sense of the New Testament certainly does not mean the elimination of human self-determination, but it does mean its sublimation; it means the ordering of human self-determination according to the order of divine predestination. In faith, at any rate, its independence *outside* of this predestination is taken away, and thus its significance *over against* God, or in *competition* with God. Its significance as the site of one's own ultimate decision is taken away and thereby certainly its character of ultimate and genuine seriousness. The only ultimate and truly serious determination of the believer is the one proceeding from Jesus Christ. Ultimately and truly he is no longer a subject because in and with his subjectivity he has become a predicate to the subject Jesus Christ, from whom he is both justified and sanctified, and receives comfort and instruction. Because the New Testament proclaims this faith, there is no room in its message for a new law that one might seek elsewhere than in the gospel itself and as such. If John the Baptist preaches about the Lamb of God who takes away the sin of the world, so he preaches along with it, and not in a second word to be heard along with this first one, repentance and amendment of life. Any independent interest in the *latter* therefore means the introduction of an alien element into the New Testament message, because the meaning of such independence can only be that 'desire' in which man would like to take back, first secretly and then openly as well, that being as a subject that was taken from him in Jesus Christ, to take back his self-determination outside of the divine predestination, and thus to leave faith behind once again. In this desire all other desires are rooted, just as the transgression of the first commandment unavoidably brings the transgression of all the others in its wake. Sin is always faithlessness. And faithlessness is always man's faith in himself. And this faith always consists in making the mystery of his responsibility into his own mystery instead of letting it be the mystery of God. It is precisely this faith that is religion. It is contradicted by the revelation witnessed to in the New Testament, just as certainly as revelation is identical with Jesus Christ as the God who acts for us and on us. This revelation characterizes religion as faithlessness.

We cannot make this statement without expressly emphasizing that it is God's *revelation* in Jesus Christ and it *alone* by which this characterization of religion as idolatry and works-righteousness, and thus its exposure as faithlessness, can really be carried out. For there is also an immanent problematic of religion that must be understood in its own right and is to be distinguished as such from the sublimation of religion by revelation. It is an observation that can be more or less clearly substantiated from the history and phenomenology of every religion: that religious man by no means approaches his theoretical and practical goal in a straight line, like one who is sure of what he is doing, but rather that in his striving for it he necessarily becomes entangled in a peculiar inner dialectic. He contradicts himself in a peculiar way, his thinking and willing at once necessarily becomes frustrated, exceeded, and surpassed by an allegedly still higher and better kind of thinking and willing, so that not only is he himself called into question, unsettled, and thrown into uncertainty, but also his whole religious enterprise is more or less radically endangered – without him thereby somehow giving up his religious concern and desire – yet also without him somehow bringing it with certainty to its goal in this new critical turn of events. If we are aware of the judgment that falls on all religion from the standpoint of revelation, then we will not marvel at this observation. For it is a confirmation of the fact that this judgment is correct: religion is always an enterprise that contradicts itself, one that is impossible in itself. But one needs to be clear that this critical turn in which the self-contradiction and impossibility of religion become visible is a moment in the life of religion itself. It has no more than immanent significance. It also does not answer conclusively or finally the question it wants to answer. It is therefore – and here is the point – not at all to be confused with revelation. The exposing of religion as faithlessness does not occur in it. Rather, this exposing befalls it as well! All religion is idolatry and works-righteousness, even at the allegedly higher stage where it seems to want to overcome idolatry and works-righteousness by its own powers and its own methods. It is a matter – to call it by its right name – of the double, though ultimately unitary, process by which the problems of religion are exposed on the one hand by *mysticism* and on the other by *atheism*. Our task is to show that religion, even in these two allegedly higher and apparently alien forms, remains utterly itself, whether for good or for ill, in success or in failure.

The two primitive and as it were common forms of all religion are, as we have seen, the representation of divinity and the fulfilment of the law. It is always in these two forms that the religious need first seeks to satisfy itself. But it *seeks* satisfaction – and this is what distinguishes the religious need from the need of the man in faith in God's revelation – because, and to the extent that, it already *has* it. For it is the need of man for a truth *above* him and for a certainty *within* him, both of which he thinks he knows and both of which he also thinks he can produce for himself. To the extent that this need is awakened in him, has not the starry heaven above him and the moral law within him[18] long since brought both, the truth and the certainty, into his horizon and province? With regard to this need he is really not at a loss for advice and help. He knows that truth and certainty *exist* and are *attainable*, and he is confident that he *can* attain them. His need is therefore not an absolute one,[19] not a strictly and purely needy need, not one in the face of which he does not know where to turn. Man in this need cannot for an instant or in any respect be compared to the neediness of the faithful man, who with empty heart and empty hands sees himself as wholly dependent on God's revelation. By marching forth boldly to grasp after the truth in order to satisfy this need – by fashioning the deity according to his own image – and with the confident act of assurance; by undertaking to justify and sanctify himself according to that which he takes to be the law, he betrays the fact that – at least potentially, at least with regard to his religious ability – by *seeking* satisfaction, he already *is* satisfied. He can be compared to a rich man who, in need of becoming richer (which of course can't be an absolute need!), puts part of his fortune into an undertaking that promises a profit.

For just this reason, first of all, a certain ultimate *non-necessity* inheres in the origin and practice of all religion. For the life of religion, in which the religious need seeks its satisfaction and provisionally finds it, is basically just an externalizing, an expression, a representation, and hence a repetition of something that was already living formlessly and fruitlessly yet nevertheless powerfully enough in the pious soul as the actual religious essence of man, and to that extent as man's actual religious possession.

> Is the necessity of religious life as expressed and represented any different from the limited, figurative, incidental, merely ornamental necessity of children's play, or of the serious or comic arts? If need be, could not religion's ideas of God remain unthought, its doctrines unarticulated, its rites and prayers unexecuted, its ascetic and moral prescriptions freely unobserved? Is the religious concern and desire really compelled to this particular expression? Is it really bound to it, once it has been created? Without this expression would it somehow cease to be what it is? The history and phenomenology of all religions shows us that this is not in fact the case: the external, the actual satisfaction of the religious need is, to be sure, a relative necessity, yet only a relative one. If need be, we can get along without the deity we have fashioned, without the justifying and sanctifying work of man.

And a second point must be added. Inherent in all the religions that have arisen and been practised, in all external satisfaction of the religious need, is a quite definite *weakness* deriving from the inner satisfaction that precedes it. For religion will never be anything more or different than a mirror image of that which man himself is and has, the man who thinks he should proceed to this external satisfaction of his need. But what will become of this mirror image when the original, religious man, becomes something different? Can religion bear to change along with man? And can it bear not to change with him?

> The religion of man is always utterly conditioned by the way in which the starry heaven above him and the moral law within him[20] have spoken precisely to *him*; hence it is conditioned by the nature and climate, by the blood and soil,[21] by the economic, cultural, political – in short, the historical – relationships in which he exists. Religion becomes an element of *custom*, by which he comes to terms with the conditions of existence imposed upon him, even apart from the question of truth and certainty – or rather, even at the lower, the penultimate stage of his enquiry into it. But these conditions of existence, and thus custom, are variable: nature and climate, or the perspective and technique with which man masters them, can change. Peoples and individuals can move. Races can mix. Here the historical relationships are completely in the grip of change, sometimes gradual, sometimes rapid, but always constant. But this means that religions are continually faced with the choice: *either* to go with the times, to change as times change, and thereby inevitably to renounce their very claim to truth and certainty; *or* else to remain behind the times, to persist in their already accomplished forms of doctrine, ritual, and community, and thereby inevitably to become old, obsolete, and fossilized; *or*, finally, to try to do both, to be a little bit liberal and a little bit conservative, in order then, with the advantages of both possibilities, necessarily to come to terms with their corresponding disadvantages. Thus it comes about that religions must fight for their lives, that they can become acutely or chronically ill: there has probably never been a religion that has not been ill, secretly or openly, from its fateful relationship to time – i.e., to human change (or rather, from their own liberalism or conservatism or both at the same time!). And it is a well-known fact that religions do also die from this illness, i.e., they can die out because of a complete lack of new believers and adherents, i.e., they can become mere historical quantities. This binding of religion to religious man in his variability is the weakness of all religion.

These two factors – the non-necessity and the weakness of all religions – constitute the precondition for that critical turn that plays a definite role in the history and shape of more or less every religion.

> The weakness of religion typically supplies the *cause*, its non-necessity the *opportunity*, for this development. In view of the changing of the times, i.e., in view of man's own variation over time, he is suddenly no longer satisfied by his previous satisfaction of the religious need, namely, as taught to him by his fathers. The features of the image of God and the norms of the law of his religion seem to him to be all too rigid or perhaps even all too fluid for him to be able any longer to feel at home in it. Its truth no longer speaks to him; its certainty

no longer holds good. Doubt stirs in him, and the desire for freedom – both are possible, since his religion, after all, possesses only that relative necessity! – and both together now seem to want to explode his inherited and accepted religion from within. He now seems to come very close – but it only seems so – to the insight that would be uttered from the standpoint of revelation concerning his religion: that he has been practising idolatry and works-righteousness, that up to now his thinking and doing have been the thinking and doing of faithlessness. Without revelation it will certainly not come to this, to the absolute crisis of his religion. For he would already have to have faith in order to be able seriously to accuse himself of faithlessness. And for him to have faith, God's revelation would already have to have encountered him. If this has not happened, then the outcome of the relative crisis into which he sees himself plunged with regard to his religion may be that a new religion with a new image of God and a new law appears on the scene, is founded and proclaimed, finds acclaim, and achieves historical scope and form in place of the old. However great the historical catastrophe may be in which such a change from religion to religion takes place, what has *not* come about is that critical turning point in which religion itself becomes problematic to man, in which the self-contradiction and impossibility of religion as such becomes visible. This radical outcome of the crisis, when it happens, is in relation to that first possibility a much quieter, much more modest, but also much more significant event. Of course, even it is not *as* radical and significant as it pretends to be. But it is without doubt more radical and significant than the dying of an old religion and emerging of a new one.

Always presupposing the actual weakness and non-necessity of religion, it can happen to a person that not only does the image of God in his religion become doubtful and its law oppressive, but that even his own corresponding activity becomes as such dubious, questionable, and impossible: the human will to form an image of God, religious dogmatics – and the human will to fulfil the law, religious morals and asceticism. It can happen to a person that the preconditions of the crisis of his religion, its weakness and its non-necessity, may become conscious in principle as factors preventing him from fleeing his previous religion into another or into a new religion because he sees plainly that the same problems await him at once there as well. Of course, it now turns out that the need that had guided him in his previous existence and activity was not a strictly and purely needy need. It was the playful need to externalize a religious possession existing prior to this externalizing and apart from it. For what a person really experiences in that crisis of his religion is merely the actual or supposed failure of this externalizing. Precisely in this externalizing he has become incredible to himself. He is no longer able or willing to participate in it, at least not inwardly or responsibly. He gives up on his religion, secretly or even openly. But in no way does he give up on the religious possession he had previously been trying to externalize, on the formless image of God that had already been living in his soul, on the fruitless self-justification and self-sanctification he had long been pursuing in his heart.

He gives up only in the sense that he now pulls back to this inward line from which he had originally started. He loses nothing by this retreat; he merely withdraws his capital from an enterprise that no longer appears profitable to him. The vitality and intensity that he had expended up to now on forming an image of God and on fulfilling the law of his religion now turn inward and are employed for the benefit and aim of that formless and fruitless reality, unthought and unwilled, out of whose richness religion first emerged, in order now to be taken back into it. The same sharpness of thought and the same power of will with which the person previously occupied himself positively and constructively when he was still credible as a religious adherent now take effect negatively and destructively. For the same religious concern and desire that previously wanted only to play, only to express and present itself, now wants instead to live out its life in non-expression, in non-presentation. The same religious need, which is not so needy at all, now seeks its satisfaction in a solemn non-satisfaction, in a passionate renunciation of representation, in a passionate silence, in a passionate coming-to-rest of the soul in itself, in the solemn emptiness that it now suddenly thinks it would prefer to its former equally solemn fullness. The thinking and willing person, however, now has his hands full differentiating this inner space, in which there are to be no more forms or works, just as there had previously been none there. His religious work now becomes one of cleaning up and clearing away in view of the anticipated abundance of life of the religious reality sounding and resounding purely within itself, which is only truly expected after the liberation from all representations. Likewise in view of this goal, any thought of a transition to another religion, or of founding a new religion, obviously becomes impossible. For that could only mean a loss of time and energy! It would be far better – and here his thinking gets its new task – to convince himself that the previously undertaken attempt at an external representation of the divine form was in itself merely a misunderstanding, in which man temporarily went astray, yet from which he nevertheless always intended and sought what is now recognized as the Real: the religious reality of the formless and fruitless inner space. And it would be better – and here even man's will is engaged anew – henceforth to concentrate all the energy once directed towards fulfilling an external law towards the task of becoming and remaining true to oneself, and in oneself to that nameless, impersonal, and non-objective will that struggles within us for truth and certainty.

This is the new road by which religious man now approaches his old theoretical-practical goal. He thinks the same thing, but now he thinks it quite differently. At any rate, he thinks he now thinks it in a radically different way. He looks down, at any rate, from a lofty vantage-point, whether indignantly or regretfully or indulgently, on those who still think it in another way than he now thinks it, and who perhaps – probably – don't even understand how very, very differently he himself now thinks it! Nevertheless, he has remained the same as himself and the other religious people, at least in the attitude, in the seriousness, in the faithful inwardness, in the enthusiasm with which he gives himself over to his cause, to the cause of the great withdrawal, to his negations and destructions, to his work of liberation – and probably also in what one calls religious fanaticism. Yet might he not have deceived himself about the utter novelty of his road? Be that as it may, we cannot fail to recognize that there has been at least a very sharp turn in the road, even if what has taken place is in principle only a continuation of the old road.

This at least relatively new religious road, which we have so far described as one, divides at a certain point and becomes the double road of *mysticism* and *atheism*. Their difference derives from their relationship to the hitherto prevailing and established religion at the time. *Mysticism*, too, signifies that man is finished with this religion practically and fundamentally as far as its expression, externalization, and representation is concerned. It signifies that he is no longer able to find truth in its image of God nor salvation and certainty in following its law.

The word 'mysticism', of course, contains a double meaning, since it can be understood as coming from *mu'ein* as well as from *muein'*. *Mu'ein* means 'to close the eyes *and* the mouth'; *muein'* means 'to consecrate'. Mysticism is that higher consecration of man that he achieves by practising the greatest possible reserve towards the external world both passively and actively. Or else it is that passive and active reserve towards the external world that is at the same time suited to a higher consecration of man.

Mysticism, too, signifies the fundamental release of man from the satisfaction of the religious need that was formerly sought on the 'outside'. But in its relationship to this 'outside', it is nevertheless the *conservative* form of that critical turn. For mysticism does not visibly attack religion, at least not initially or at the outset. It does not negate it directly. It has no interest in iconoclasm, the denial of dogma, or similar open acts of liberation. It submits to the prevailing doctrine and observance, and it may even respect them. It is content to let religion stand. In some cases it is even in a position seemingly to enrich its dogmatics through certain especially profound and serious pronouncements, and its worship through certain especially meaningful forms (mysteries), and seemingly to give wholly new life to the general religious community through especially impressive representation of its principles and by specially gathering and training the most faithful among its faithful. It gladly and honestly presents itself as the true 'friendship with God'.[22] The radicalness of the withdrawal from the external religious position is basically effective in its mystical form only in so far as the mystic wants to have everything that is taught and practised in a particular religion understood inwardly, spiritually, vitally – i.e., in relation to the reality of that formless and fruitless inner space and not in its abstract externality. The mystic will emphasize and stress the fact that everything external is mere image and form, that everything transitory is only a likeness, that it has its truth only in its relation to the inexpressible, because non-objective, essence from which it emerged and to which it must also return again. The specifically mystical passion for renunciation, for silence, for the way of quietude is directed towards understanding, explaining, interpreting the external, which still remains valid and must be respected. The mystic will always say even the most dangerous things – e.g., about the secret identity of inner and outer, of the ego and God – very piously, and always in connection with the religious tradition, which apparently asserts the opposite. He will seek to make the tradition, so to speak, into a witness against itself. He will claim the freedom only for this *interpretation* of the tradition, never the freedom simply to *abolish* the tradition. We should not be surprised if he far exceeds ordinary believers in outward conservatism! And he does all this not, as people so often accuse him, out of human fear or untruthfulness, but rather because in his own way he sincerely loves the tradition, the entire system of religion as expressed outwardly. For he loves it because he quite simply *needs* it: as the text for his interpretations, as material for his spiritualizing, as the external realm that he must internalize, as the point of departure for the great withdrawal in which, according to him, knowledge of the truth takes place. What would mysticism be without its counterpart, religious dogmatics and ethics? If the latter were to perish, mysticism would have to 'give up the ghost for want', just as it asserts God would have to do in case man should perish! In fact, mysticism lives by this counterpart, and it therefore tends to treat it gently, and with great tenderness.

It therefore signifies no contradiction whatever and must not be interpreted as an aberration when Johann Scheffler, for example, after allowing the ego and God to be wholly absorbed and annihilated in one another, could suddenly also sing,

> Claim not wisdom for thyself, however bright thou art,
> Only the Catholic Christian has God's wisdom in his heart,

or when he expressed himself in like manner over a wide range of his poetical work. 'This sensitive bard, who came to dogmatics out of a profound vision, who knocked at the door, who thought he could move stones with the eyes of a seer, who wanted to make dried-up grain green again by throwing himself into the thorns, into the dead undergrowth with breast bared – now *he* experienced something! Out of the thornbush crept a spider that sucked his heart's blood dry. And suddenly he was hanging in the thorns, himself like soulless dry grain. The wind touched it: it sang on, in a final indestructible echo of its loving power. Intermingled with it, however, were odious rattling sounds of the ghostly branch.

Scheffler became an orthodox fanatic ...'[23] Even devotees of a radical mysticism cannot judge more ignorantly! As though mysticism did not demand precisely the complement of the prevailing and accepted religion! What is it supposed to dismantle, hollow out, reduce, negate, when such a religion no longer exists? It is precisely in the genius, the prudence and economy, with which Angelus Silesius advocated and advanced the mystical cause, that one can see that he too was engaged as an 'orthodox fanatic' – along with many comrades in China, in India, in Arabia, and much more intelligently than his admirers in the modern West!

From this aspect, at least, one might well call *atheism*, in its relation to existing religion, the impulsive, puerile form of that critical turn. Atheism means, first of all, that the secret is out: this turn, in so far as it can be 'about' anything, is simply about *negation*. Certainly atheism too, even in its most radical forms, ultimately intends something positive, and in fact the same positive that is also intended in mysticism: the religious reality in the formless and fruitless inner space, where knowledge and object are still, or again, one – the Chinese *Tao*, the Indian *Tat twam asi*, the Hegelian in-and-for-itself of the absolute spirit. Mysticism too must negate and intends to negate for the sake of this positive; it too can finally only say no; for it too existing religion with its dogmatics and ethics is basically just a building condemned to demolition. But mysticism will, so far as possible, do it under cover and in silence. Atheism, however, shouts it aloud to the world. It hurls itself against religion in open conflict. It loves iconoclasm, the denial of dogma, and of course moral emancipation. It negates the existence of God and the validity of a divine law. And it invests all its passion precisely in this negation as such. Therein lies its complete heedlessness. It overlooks what mysticism does not overlook: that absolute negation makes sense only against the background of a relative affirmation; that the herd cannot continually be slaughtered unless it is periodically fed and tended, or at least protected. It lives in and by its 'no'; it knows only how to demolish and clear away, and thereby exposes itself to the danger that sooner or later it will be running on empty. But there is also a second consideration: atheism sets out to be purer and more consistent than mysticism as the negation of *religion as such*, its God and its law. In the case of atheism there is more plainly evident than in mysticism the sense of the common critical turn as a retreat from the religious dogma of truth and way of certainty, devised and maintained by man, yet no longer credible to that very same man. Atheism, more energetic than mysticism intensively, is more modest extensively. It is content to deny God and his law, thereby overlooking the fact that outside of religion there are quite different dogmas of truth and ways of certainty that can at any moment take on just as religious a character. Mysticism is also in this respect the cleverer, more circumspect undertaking: sooner or later it extends to everything; it calls into question not only God but also, to be on the safe side, the cosmos and the self as well. It designs and executes a programme of comprehensive negation and thereby covers its back, or at least it thinks it can do so. Atheism, on the other hand, does not deny the reality of nature, history and culture, the animal and rational existence of man, this or that morality or even immorality. On the contrary, those are the authorities and powers to which the atheist is in the habit of giving himself over in the most cheerful and naive credibility. Atheism almost always means secularism. And moreover, atheism is in the habit of allying itself with precisely these secular authorities and powers in the struggle against religion, against God and his law. Atheism argues by assuming their existence and validity; they are for it the unshakable conditions, on the basis of which it raises the objection against the religious authorities and powers that they are nothing. It is clear that in so doing it exposes itself to the danger that behind its back, and possibly with its confirmation, all sorts of disguised, and perhaps even undisguised, new religions can arise.

Precisely in this double unprotectedness, atheism is nevertheless the more original, undiminished, and ultimately powerful form of the critical turn that we are dealing with here. The meaning of this turn is here *negation* pure and simple, and in fact, specifically and concretely, the negation of the *religious superworld*, which is identifiable by its weakness and non-necessity, and which has become superfluous and tiresome as a result of some kind of change in the conditions of human existence. In essence, of course, mysticism too is negation in ever new forms and degrees. It too cannot speak of the positive that it allegedly intends – the glory of the inner space that absorbs everything external into itself – otherwise than in negations. And simply to ensure that it does not run out of material for this enterprise, it manifests a certain forbearance, or even encouragement, of the religious positions themselves. And mysticism, too, though it goes about its work more comprehensively, intends in the final analysis, specifically and concretely, the negation of the religious superworld. This realm, and not the cosmos, and also not the self, is really the ultimate external to be internalized – i.e., negated. Mysticism is esoteric atheism. But atheism nevertheless carries the banner and the laurels in the work of liberation which is their common purpose. If their common programme can be carried out, then along with the disadvantage of a lesser wisdom, atheism has the advantage of a more direct and consistent approach. If only it did not at the same time betray the fact that the common programme can*not* be carried out! But the fact that it cannot be carried out shows up in two questions that cannot be answered: (1) Where does the negation of the religious superworld as such really lead in the end? And (2) How can the emergence of new, disguised superworlds really be effectively controlled? Can the critical turn in religion – a mysticism aiming at atheism, and an atheism interpreting mysticism (that great master of interpretation!) – lead anywhere but to nowhere? And in practical terms that surely means that it will lead either to the practice of the old religions once again, or to the formation of new ones.

> Whenever the atheist recognizes the danger of the sterile negation in which he finds himself, then at the very last moment he usually borrows from his wiser and more reserved partner. Thus the great work that F. Mauthner wrote in honour of Western atheism concludes with a section entitled 'The Peace of Godless Mysticism',[24] in which at the very end he comes to speak once again of a 'concept of God purified of the rubbish of theologians', which Mauthner will permit his readers, provided they think of it as no more than a 'normal deception, a healthy vital lie, an unavoidable lifelong illusion', provided they do not wish to say Yes to it. This concept of God is supposed to consist of nothing more than a 'stammering "something"' (p. 446). One might think this permission all too meagre. One might also be of the opinion, however, that precisely in this 'stammering something' all idolatry and works-righteousness have their beginning. One might also be of the opinion that basically with this permission, despite all the protests, the door is thrown open once again to every conceivable religious splendour. For if the atheist can no longer hold out as a pure atheist, if he wants once again to become a mystic, then let him beware lest in time he inevitably also become a dogmatician and ethicist once more, after the model of Angelus Silesius!
>
> And what if the atheist recognizes his other danger: that even after accomplishing the negation of the God of religion and his law, new deities may be free to rear their heads out of the nature, culture, and history that has not been negated, and out of man's own animal and rational existence? Well, then perhaps with Otto Petras (*Post Christum*, 1936) he may do the following: he may issue a decree to himself and others (on the basis of some philosophy of history or other) that today all ideologies and mythologies, not just this or that one, are dead, finally dead, dead once and for all; that for the man of our time all that remains is the venture, spurning every dream of a superworld, of a naked, endangered, and death-confronting existence, callous in every regard. Such an existence is already realized in the figure of certain soldiers in the World War, in the figure of the ocean flyer cruising along in the infinite between heaven and earth, or in the figure of this or that daring modern knight of industry – the figure of the man devoid of all illusions, hopes, and fears, who marches on, knowing not whence nor whither, simply for the sake of marching. Very well! But then the dilemma arises. Either this new form of existence is only lived but not preached by whatever individuals are pleased to bow to this new decree. In that case atheism becomes a private affair, and that's the end of its critical function towards religion. Or else this new form of existence is not only lived but also publicly proclaimed. In that case it too will not be able to do without some foundational and explanatory ideology and mythology – i.e., for it too some kind of superworld will have to be dreamed up – and here too the critical turn against religion has become the formation of a new religion – or perhaps even the confirmation of an old one.

To summarize: the critical turn against religion indeed signifies the exposure of its weakness and merely relative necessity. In its mystical form, however, it cannot avoid combining its negation with an affirmation of religion that is certainly not naive but is nevertheless an affirmation. And if in its atheistic form it should want to escape this consequence, it cannot avoid, unwillingly but in fact, opening up a broad field for new forms of religion, if not actually preparing it. That means, however, that the critical turn against religion, even in these two most principled forms, is not so radical and powerful that it can make clear, even just in theory, how it actually intends to carry out the negation of religion, its god and its law. The will and intent are plain, but the way is not. Historically we must also say that the religions, with their inherent ability to be both conservative and liberal, have so far proven in comparison to mysticism as well as atheism to have greater staying power, more viable resources. Historically, if a religion died, then it died because of the victory of another religion and not because of the objectively more principled attack of mysticism or atheism. So in fact even the weakness and the merely conditional necessity of religion are not so fatally effective as they might be. In its weakness and its merely condi-tional necessity religion appears in changing forms again and again, and mysticism and atheism are finally not even in a position to show how and in what way it could be otherwise, because in their own existence they are so bound up with the existence of religion.

And finally, if we could imagine the unimaginable (and, according to all historical experience, improbable), the historical existence of a pure mysticism, which would have to be identical with that of a pure atheism, then this purity would obviously consist in the fact that the negation, which after all is supposed to be only a means to an end, only a work of liberation, the dangerous negation – dangerous, namely, to mysticism and atheism themselves – which as such is nevertheless suited to bring religion on to the scene in one way or another, [that this negation] had finally achieved its goal. Man would then finally, once and for all, be free of God and his law, free of all religious works and all religious activity, free of all his striving for expression and representation, free to be really happy in that formless and fruitless inner space, happy by himself and thus simultaneously happy by himself in the real world beyond the opposition of inner and outer. Why should there not always have been mystically or atheistically inclined individuals who could at least imagine themselves to be happy in this way? They might well have tasted and felt the great positive, which is, after all, intended in the whole critical turn against religion, and from which alone its negations could have their relative power, and without which mysticism and atheism are always in danger of betrayal to religion. But what about this positive? It is not really as opposed to religion as its few fortunate and countless unfortunate devotees are in the habit of assuring us. It is actually opposed to religion only in the way that the spring is opposed to the stream, or the root to the tree, or the unborn child in the womb to the fully grown adult. It is the quiet religious possession; it is the intuition of the universe and the creative power of the individual feeling that strives to grasp it in its nameless, formless, and fruitless unity; it is the capacity to be in the world and to be human, which always precedes the 'stammering "something"' but which for sure will quickly enough project out of itself first this 'stammering "something"' and then some kind of religion or other. Precisely this capacity to be in the world and to be human is, as man's own capacity, identical with the capacity to devise and fashion gods and to justify and sanctify himself. This capacity, and therefore the great positive beyond all the negations, and therefore the happiness that the presence and enjoyment of this positive is able to produce, and therefore (if there has ever been or will ever be such a thing) pure mysticism or pure atheism – none of these can ever be the real crisis of religion. This capacity itself belongs within the magic circle of religion – and belongs there as the creative and organizing centre, even as the actual point of origin.

> Whoever does not wish to accept this proposition, let him read its immortal proof in Schleiermacher's *Speeches on Religion* ('To the Educated Among Its Despisers'), 1799. He was right, not only as an apologist but as an expert expositor of religion, not to believe the despising of the all too uneducated, but rather to address them boldly in the name of the God 'who will be in you'.

A real crisis of religion would have to strike at this capacity too, and in fact to do so at the outset and decisively. Not satisfied with the cheap successes to be achieved against the temple buildings, ceremonies, and observances, against the theologies, ideologies, and mythologies of external religion, a real crisis of religion would have to shout into that inner room: *Here* is the 'factory of idols'! *Here* lying, murdering, stealing, and harlotry are committed! *Here* one rightly cries, *Écrasez l'infâme!*[25] Here or nowhere; for if it doesn't happen here, then from this very point religion and the religions will surely grow back like the heads of the Lernaean Hydra,[26] however zealously one may on the outside deny God and break his law. Whether mystical or atheistic, any turning against the religions that would be capable of this drastic judgment against religion is obviously impossible, because in making this judgment it would also be directing it against itself. One can say categorically that it will not appear on the scene in the future any more than it has in the past. Only from a place outside the magic circle of religion, along with its place of origin – that is, only from a place outside of man – could this real crisis of religion break in. Only in an opposition wholly other than that between religion and the religious capacity, only from the standpoint of faith, could the verdict 'faithlessness, idolatry, works-righteousness' strike at this whole sphere, and thus at the whole man, in such a way that he could no longer flee from one refuge into another. In God's revelation this does happen, to be sure. In the meantime, however, provided this doesn't happen, religion and the religions can rest at ease. There can be no doubt that, with a certain change but also with a certain persistence, religion and religions will reappear again and again. A certain anxiety caused by mystics and atheists from time to time and within certain limits – whenever a greater or lesser historical upheaval is due – likewise belongs to the innermost life of religion, just as do its positive expressions and representations, the deities and laws against which the mystical and atheistic critique is directed. The ebb as much as the flow, after all, belongs to the innermost life of the ocean. And precisely in their increasingly pure forms – to the extent they are even possible – this critical turn will assuredly be harmless to religion.

> For to the extent that the purity of mysticism and atheism increases, that the work of liberation approaches its goal in particular individuals, and that they actually, or else allegedly and presumably, achieve peace in the positive sense that is intended in the whole matter – to that extent their aggressiveness towards religion and the religions will certainly decrease. All the great 'friends of God' and 'deniers of God' have at least managed ultimately to reach a kind of tolerance towards religion, thus confirming once again that the mother can never wholly deny her child.

That sublimation of religion, however, which signifies a real and dangerous assault upon it is found in another book, in comparison to which the books of mysticism and atheism can only be described as utterly harmless.

3. THE TRUE RELIGION

Our investigations so far have led to the conclusion that we can talk about 'true' religion only in the sense in which we talk about a 'justified sinner'.

Religion is never and nowhere true as such and in itself. On the contrary, the claim that it is true – i.e., that it is in truth the knowledge and worship of God and the reconciliation of man with God – is denied to every religion by God's revelation for the reason that God's revelation, as God's self-offering and self-presentation, as the work of the peace concluded by God himself between him and man, is the truth, beside which there is no other, over against which there is only falsehood and wrong. If the concept of a 'true religion' is supposed to mean a truth belonging to one religion as such and in itself, it is as incapable of being realized as the concept of a 'good man', if his goodness is supposed to signify something of which he is capable out of his own ability. No religion *is* true. A religion can only *become* true – i.e., correspond to that which it purports to be and wants people to take it to be. And this happens in precisely the same way that man is justified: only *from without*, that is, not out of its own essence and being, but only by virtue of an accounting, acceptance, and distinction that is alien to its own essence and being, inconceivable from its own standpoint, something that happens to it quite apart from any aptitude or merit. Like the justified man, the true religion is a creature of *grace*. That grace, however, is God's revelation, the same one before which no religion can stand as a true religion, the same one before which no man is justified, the same one that subjects us to the judgment of death. But just as it can call the dead to life and sinners to repentance, it can also create true religion, right in the midst of that great sphere where, seen from its standpoint, there is only false religion. The sublimation of religion by revelation does not only have to mean its negation, not only the judgment that religion is faithlessness. Religion, even though that judgment upon it is valid, and for that very reason, can be *happily* sublimated in revelation, it can be sustained by it and rest secure within it; religion can be justified by revelation and – we must immediately add – sanctified. Revelation can accept religion and single it out as true religion. And that is not all it can do. How could we have come to assert that it could do it, unless it had already done it? There is a true religion: just as there are justified sinners. As long as we remain strictly and precisely within this analogy – and it is more than an analogy, for in the broad sense it is the very matter that we are dealing with here – we must not hesitate to state that *the Christian religion is the true religion*.

In our reflections on 'Religion as Faithlessness' we deliberately left out of consideration the difference between Christian and non-Christian religion, in the sure conviction that the Christian religion as such was equally affected by everything that was to be said there. In the context of these reflections it was not possible to speak of Christianity in particular;

it was not possible to attribute to Christianity a special position, a place protected from every judgment. These reflections could not, therefore, be understood as a polemic against the non-Christian religions that might have served as preparation for the proposition that the Christian religion is the true religion, so that our only further task would be to show that the Christian religion, in contrast to the non-Christian ones, is not guilty of idolatry and works-righteousness, hence is not faithlessness but faith, and hence the true religion – or to show (which comes to the same thing in the end) that the Christian religion is not a religion at all but rather that, in contrast to all religions, including their mystical and atheistic self-criticism, it is in itself the correct and holy, thus the irreproachable and indisputable, form of communion between God and man. We could have taken this approach, however, only by simultaneously denying the very thing that must be affirmed here. The proposition that the Christian religion is the true religion, if it is to be a substantive proposition, may be ventured only in listening to God's revelation. But a proposition ventured in listening to God's revelation can only be a proposition of faith. A proposition of faith, however, must be a proposition conceived and uttered in faith and from faith, but that means in acknowledgment of and with regard to that which is said to us through revelation. Its explicit and implicit content will have to be wholly determined by that which is said to us. That, however, would precisely not be the case if we tried to reach the proposition that the Christian religion is the true religion by an approach in which, at the outset, we would leave behind the judgment of revelation that religion is faithlessness as a matter of no concern to us as Christians, in order to employ it only against other people, the non-Christians, and with the help of this judgment to separate and distinguish ourselves from them. Rather, it is incumbent on us precisely as Christians to allow this judgment to apply first and most acutely to ourselves, and to the others, the non-Christians, only to the extent that we recognize ourselves in them – i.e., to the extent that we recognize that the truth of this judgment of revelation applies to us and encounters us – and thus in a solidarity in which we, anticipating them in both repentance and hope, submit ourselves to this judgment, in order thereby also to participate in the promise of revelation. If we follow this way to the end, it will bring us to the promise, for those who submit themselves to God's judgment and allow themselves to be found guilty of faithlessness – it will bring us to faith in this promise, and in this faith to the presence and reality of God's grace, which does indeed distinguish our religion, the Christian religion, from all the others as *the true religion*. Only in this utterly humble way can this utterly lofty goal be achieved. And it would not be the truly humble way unless we undertook it in the awareness that here any 'achievement' can consist only in the utterly modest and grateful acceptance of a state of affairs that we would not achieve unless it had already been achieved in God's revelation before we set out on the way.

3. The True Religion

So it remains the case that the knowledge of the truth of the Christian religion begins with the acknowledgment that it too stands under the judgment that religion is faithlessness, and that it is acquitted of this judgment not by its own inner worthiness but only by God's grace, proclaimed and effective in his revelation. This judgment, however, refers concretely to all the activity of our faith – our Christian ideas of God and divine things; our Christian theology; our Christian worship of God; our forms of Christian community and order; our Christian morality, poetry, and art; our attempts at shaping individual and social Christian life; our Christian strategy and tactics in the interest of our Christian cause – in short, our *Christianity*, just to the extent that it is *our* Christianity, a human work undertaken by us and applied to various short- and long-term goals, which as such appears on the same level with the human works of other religions. All this activity of faith, in general and in particular, is not what it intends and pretends to be, a work of faith and therefore of obedience to God's revelation; rather, what we have here – in its own way, a different way from the rest of religion, but in its own way no less seriously – is human faithlessness, i.e., opposition to God's revelation and therefore idolatry and works-righteousness both in intent and in action. With the same impotence and high-handedness, with the same lofty humanity that signifies its profound lostness, one here overlooks and opposes God's self-presentation and self-offering, the reconciliation accomplished by him, disregarding the divine consolations and prophecies, erecting great and small towers of Babel, which therefore most certainly cannot be pleasing to God, just as they are also most certainly not erected to his glory.

In order to see how self-evident this observation is for Holy Scripture, one need only attend to all those contexts in which the people of Israel or the New Testament community of disciples also occasionally appear abstractly in their human existence – as this people, as this community, to be sure, but for an instant, as it were, behind the back of Yahweh or of Jesus Christ. We can think of Exod. 32, the scene at the foot of Mt Sinai that follows immediately after the conclusion of the covenant and the giving of the law: Israel, the community of Yahweh, the people of the revelation under the leadership of Aaron, the head of its priesthood, in the full performance of his religion! It is just that Moses is missing for a while and with him evidently also the concrete gracious presence of Yahweh, which would make this religion true. The result: a 'festival of Yahweh', as expressly stated in v. 5, is being celebrated, to be sure; but behold! – it consists in worship and sacrifice before the graven image of a calf. In undeniable devotional zeal they have all contributed their best to it. Aaron himself designed and made it. 'And they shouted: Here is the God, O Israel, that led you out of Egypt!' (v. 4). 'And Yahweh spoke to Moses: I see now that this people is a stiff-necked people. So leave me now, that my wrath may burn hot against them and I may consume them ...' (v. 10). That is the religion of revelation as such, the religion of revelation seen in its reality, abstracted even just for an instant from the grace of revelation! Above all, the prophet Amos obviously saw things quite similarly when he uses the blunt word 'transgressions' to describe the sacrifice to Yahweh brought to Bethel and Gilgal (4:4). Or when he plainly warns, 'Do not seek Bethel, and do not enter into Gilgal!' (5:5). Or when he proclaims in the name of Yahweh: 'I hate, I despise your feasts, and I take no delight in your solemn assemblies. Even though you offer me your burnt offerings and cereal offerings, I will not accept them, and the peace offerings of your fatted beasts I will not look upon. Take away from me the noise of your songs; to the melody of your harps I will not listen' (5:21–3). Or when in bitter earnest he raises the question, 'Did you bring to me sacrifices and offerings the forty years in the wilderness?' (5:25) and explicitly also the question that devastatingly relativizes Israel's whole existence: '"Are you not like the Ethiopians to me, O people of Israel?" is the word of Yahweh. "Did I not bring up Israel from the land of Egypt, and the Philistines from Caphtor and the Syrians from Kir?"' (9:7). After all this, one can easily understand why the priest Amaziah believed he should denounce this man to the king as a 'conspirator' and expel him from the royal temple of Bethel (7:10–13); and it is equally significant that Amos expressly refuses to be a prophet or of the prophetic guild (7:14–15). For Amos an irreconcilable contradiction appears to open up between revelation and the religion of revelation. We also see in Isa. 1:11f., Jer. 6:20f., and Ps. 50:7f. the same exposure of nakedness, of inner disobedience, and in reality even of the religion of revelation in its human practice. In Jer. 7:21f. it can be intensified to this acerbic opposition: 'Add your burnt offerings to your sacrifices, and eat the flesh. For in the day that I brought them out of the land of Egypt, I did not speak to your fathers or command them concerning burnt offerings and sacrifices. But this command I gave them, 'Obey my voice, and I will be your God, and you shall be my people; and walk in all the way that I command you, that it may be well with you.' And Jer. 8:8f.: 'How can you say, "We are wise, and the law of Yahweh is with us"? But behold, the false pen of the scribes has made it into a lie. The wise men shall be put to shame, they shall be dismayed and taken; lo, they have rejected the word of Yahweh, and what wisdom is in them?'

One understands such pointed statements rightly, however, only in the context of the prophetic critique and preaching of repentance and judgment in general. Of course, this critique also belongs to the life of Old Testament religion as such; it is also directed immanently against religious apostasy, against the distortion and degeneration of this religion, against cultic disloyalty and moral decadence. But is not the phenomenal breadth of its form and the incomparably radical nature of its accusations, judgments, and threats really only understandable when one sees that it always has to do here with something other than opposition to this or that concrete aberration or sin of Israel, though of course these are certainly also to be taken seriously? Rather, at every point it has to do also with the necessary struggle of revelation against the religion of revelation, a struggle in which the prophets truly did not spare even prophecy itself. Is it not as though the entire religion of Israel were being crushed between two millstones: between *one* word of God that establishes, orders, and shapes it in all its specificity; and *another* word of God by which, one might almost say, every concrete act of obedience to this commandment is exposed in the same specificity as faithlessness? Might one not ask whether in this dreadful process an injustice has been done to this obviously deeply and seriously religious people, which despite all delusions and confusions has nevertheless held on to its religion tenaciously for a millennium under the most difficult circumstances? One will not ask this question, one will understand the whole process – for the Old Testament has exemplary significance in this regard as well – if one sees that in this process revelation's judgment of religion as such does in fact fall directly upon the religion of revelation. But for just this reason this process can, indeed must, also conclude almost as a matter or course with the promise of salvation, which is so difficult to explain psychologically and historically. It really has nothing to do with a sentimental mood of sunset after the storm. It belongs so necessarily together with the word of judgment, because the word of judgment so profoundly concerns the whole. It announces God's incomprehensible verdict of acquittal. It announces that here those who were chastised, God loves, that those who died shall live. For the word remains constant, and the covenant of Yahweh, often broken and defiled, remains constant; and so Israel remains the people of revelation and its religion the religion of revelation. Until Jesus Christ, that is, by whose rejection Israel committed not just this or that sin as before, by which it not only broke and defiled the word and the covenant, but rather denied and abandoned it in substance. Once more, and this time comprehensively, Israel's fate becomes exemplary: *the religion of revelation is indeed bound to God's revelation; but God's revelation is not bound to the religion of revelation.* The prophetic critique of religion is now seen to be predictive: the abstraction that for a thousand years had only stood threateningly on the horizon as a burning question has now come to pass; what at one time had become visible on occasion, each time overcome by the opposing aspect, is now apparent in all its nakedness: a human religion, once the human answer to revelation required and ordered by God, accused and condemned in its exercise as faithlessness and yet always accepted again in grace, but now – this example too had to be recorded – but now a religion rejected, emptied, because robbed of its ground and object, now the Jewish religion, from which God has turned away his countenance, one among many others and no more than they! It has just one advantage over the others, and it is something terrible: the fact that it was once more than they but was ultimately just the same as all the rest. So utterly is it the case that only by the grace of God the true religion is the true one, that it must allow itself to by exposed and condemned by grace as false religion; and if it rejects that very grace, and thereby its unmerited acquittal, it can be nothing more than false religion, faithlessness, idolatry, and works-righteousness. The church, if it knows what it is doing when it take its own religion, the Christian religion, to be the true one, must never lose sight of this example, never cease hearing the warnings of Amos and Jeremiah.

And it is no different in the New Testament. At times the disciples can be seen in their humanity – apart, as it were, from their commission and from the directing and sustaining word of Jesus, the disciples on this side of Easter and Pentecost, standing for a moment on their own feet. In such cases, they too, in a transition no less abrupt than Israel's in the Old Testament and obviously subject to the same order, enter at once into those strange shadows where their religion too becomes recognizable, and likewise recognizable as faithlessness. Here the exemplary figure is above all the apostle Peter. The Roman Church would be right in its claim to be the successor to this particular disciple if it had paid just a little more attention to his role. Whenever Peter stands on his own feet, he is precisely the one whose intentions are not divine but human (Mt. 16:23), the doubter who ventures forth only to fail at once (Mt. 14:28f.), who can cut off Malchus' right ear (Jn 18:10) but then also deny Jesus three times, to whom Jesus once says very unambiguously: when you have turned again, strengthen your brethren (Lk. 22:32). But what strange figures the other disciples also constantly cut. We may think of the recurrent question of who is the greatest in the kingdom of heaven (Mt. 18:1); or of the sons of Zebedee with their wish to sit at Jesus' right and left hand (Mk 10:35f.); or of the despair of the disciples in the storm at sea – 'Why are you afraid? Have you no faith?' (Mk 4:35f.) – or of their sleep in the Garden of Gethsemane (Mk 14:37f.); or of their presumption and their perplexity in so many other cases. 'Behold, Satan demanded to have you, that he might sift you like wheat' (Lk. 22:31). There can be no doubt: it is not a matter of particular cases, perhaps very frequent, of omission and error by the disciples, but rather of the most fundamental thing, that they – although and because Jesus has called them, although and because they follow him – are members of a *genea apistos* ('faithless generation', Mk 9:19), are utterly outside although and because they are utterly inside. Whenever they stand on their own feet, and to the extent that they do – as is quite clear in the four gospels – they are always utterly outside. It is clear that they have religion, but it is just as clear that their religion is faithlessness. Whenever it is otherwise, as becomes evident for instance in Peter's confession (Mt. 16:13f.) or in the confession of Thomas (Jn 20:24f.), then this other is immediately identified as grace. *Me ginou apistos, alla pistos* ('Do not be faithless but faithful'), the resurrected Jesus says to Thomas while letting him touch his wounds (Jn 20:27). We have an explicit explanation of this situation in Jn 15:1f.: the disciples are branches of Jesus Christ, the vine. If a branch bears no fruit, it will be cut off. If it bears fruit, it will be pruned, that it may bear more fruit. 'You are already made clean by the word which I have spoken to you. Abide in me, and I in you. As the branch cannot bear fruit by itself, unless it abides in the vine, neither can you, unless you abide in me. I am the vine, you are the branches. He who abides in me, and I in him, he it is that bears much fruit, for apart from me you can do nothing (*choris emou ou dunasthe poiein ouden*). If a man does not abide in me, he is cast forth as a branch and withers; and the branches are gathered, thrown into the fire and burned.' The Acts of the Apostles then shows us the deeds of these same disciples, now as apostles, now as fruit-bearing branches on the vine. Precisely this 'on the vine', however, must not be overlooked, and the reminder that 'apart from me you can do nothing' must not be misappropriated, if the Christian religion, presenting itself unambiguously as the true religion in person, is now to confront the false religions of the Jews and pagans. For it is not its person but its office that is distinguished in this way; it is the outpouring of the Holy Spirit that offers the indispensable key to this story. As always, it is possible that the Christian religion too, unless it is faith through God's grace, can be faithlessness, as shown for instance in the figures of Ananias and Sapphira (Acts 5:1f.), in the figure of Simon Magus (Acts 8:13f.), and in a somewhat different way also in the disciples of John at Ephesus (Acts 19:1f.). From the apostolic epistles we should above all mention 1 Cor. 13 (where the concept of 'love' would surely be understood best if it were simply replaced by the name Jesus Christ!). The entire inventory of religion of a living Christian congregation in Paul's time is enumerated there: speaking in tongues, prophecy, understanding mysteries, a faith that moves mountains, giving away one's possessions to the poor right up to the last, finally martyrdom in the flames – and it is said of all of them that they do not help the Christian, not at all, unless he has love. For love alone never ends, while prophecy, speaking in tongues, *gnosis*[1] will be 'sublimated'.[2] Their work remains incomplete, for it lacks the whole and therefore lacks everything; it is childish thinking that must cease, indirect contemplation in a mirror. In the midst of the apostolic witness (which also truly holds the Christian religion to be the true religion), the Christian religion could not be more comprehensively relativized in favour of revelation, which also means the crisis precisely of the religion of revelation.

Now this relativizing of the Christian religion does not mean that the Christian faith should become disheartened, insecure, or weak; nor that even the decision for the truth of the Christian religion might thereby be robbed of its power or confidence. For the Christian faith does not live by the self-confidence with which the Christian can distinguish himself from the non-Christian. There is such a self-confidence, of course, and in its place it is even right and necessary. This self-confidence, however, also has its natural limit: it cannot possibly mean that the Christian could want to assert himself over against God in a righteousness and holiness of his own. It will be wholly unbroken in relation to men, and wholly broken in relation to God; and because it is wholly broken in the latter case, it will be wholly unbroken in the former.

Here one may refer by way of comparison to what Paul writes in 1 Cor. 4:2f. about his response to the judgment brought against him in Corinth. Not only is he not afraid of being charged by the Corinthians or any other human tribunal; he also does not think of bringing charges against himself (*ouden gar emauto sunoida*, 'I am not aware of anything against myself') – truly an unbroken self-confidence! 'But I am not thereby justified. It is the Lord who judges me ... He will bring to light the things now hidden in darkness and will disclose the purposes of the heart. Then every man will receive his commendation from God.' Even the apostolic self-confidence, which remains so unbroken over against men, is thus subject to this brokenness.

Accordingly, in Rom. 4:1f. Paul did not simply deny to Abraham as the father of Israel and all the faithful a 'justification by works' and a corresponding *kauchema* ('something to boast about'), but he did point out that according to the word of scripture it could not be a matter of some glory before God, but that Abraham's justification before God was rather the justification of a godless man, and his faith the faith in this justification and therefore not his trust in his works, in circumcision and law – in short, not in his religious self-confidence.

Knowledge of the relativizing of even the Christian religion by God's revelation has to do with just this delimiting of religious self-confidence.

This delimiting comes about in faith and through faith. So how could it mean a weakening of faith? Rather, faith will prove its *power* – and the Christian will *live* precisely in the power of his faith – by the fact that faith continually forces him to think beyond his religious self-confidence, and so constantly to take into account the relativizing of his Christian religion by God's revelation. And it should be noted that from this standpoint, and only from this standpoint, can the decision for the truth of the Christian religion be taken with real power. The only strong human positions are always the ones that are entirely abandoned before God – that is, positions seen to be entirely untenable when measured by his will and judgment. Also with regard to our own being and acting, we never behave wisely, but always unwisely, whenever we try to take refuge from God and make ourselves secure in some nook or cranny of our being and acting. Not only our security before God, but also the very security of our being and acting, and so also our security in relation to men, rests absolutely on our willingness, in faith and by faith, to deny ourselves such forms of security.

Here we need to recall the remarkable passage in 2 Cor. 12:1f. Without a doubt Paul speaks here not only, as in 1 Cor. 13, about the religion of the Christian community but rather in highly personal terms about his own most intimate religious experience. In this area there are great things about which he could 'boast', and he might even do so without speaking foolishly but in truth. He has been granted *optasiai kai apokalupseis* ('visions and revelations'), and in particular 'fourteen years ago' a rapture into the third heaven, into paradise, including hearing 'words that cannot be told', which no man may utter. But who really is the one who might boast of all these things? Paul speaks three times (vv. 2, 3, 5) as of someone else: 'I know a man ...' He calls him a 'man in Christ'. He doubtless means himself. However – and this is what is significant in the description of this ecstasy – he nevertheless distances himself from him, and only from this distance is he willing to participate in the glory that this man – he himself! – has from those high things. 'Of this man's glory I will boast, but of *my own* glory I will *not* boast, except of my weaknesses' (v. 5 according to Schlatter). But he is kept from hubris with regard to that experience (v. 7) and forced paradoxically to boast of his weakness by the fact that, like a thorn in his flesh, an angel of Satan stands at his side harassing him. He cannot be chased away by even the most earnest prayer to Jesus Christ, and Paul evidently no longer wishes to chase him away; rather, where he is present and active Paul now catches sight formally of the order in whose power he is held fast outside the circle of those experiences: where the power of Christ dwells with him, that is, in his weakness. For the Lord's answer to his prayer is *arkei soi he charis mou; he gar dunamis en astheveia teleitai* ('My grace is sufficient for you, for my power is made perfect in weakness', v. 9). So he wishes to boast of his weakness and it alone: 'For when I am weak, then I am strong.' But what is his weakness? Simply what remains of his Christian existence after it is stripped of the religious experience of which he could boast for good reason and in truth, but that means insults, hardships, persecutions, calamities for Christ's sake (v. 10). There he sees the *power* of Christ dwelling in him; there he knows himself to be *strong*; there is what he *boasts* about. And one can study precisely in Paul's case how the true security of his being and acting, how the power of his decision, how the firmness of his position even towards the outside, how completely the *energy* of his religious self-confidence in relation to the other – how all this is rooted in the fact that he allows everything, the Christian religion – *in concreto* his special 'revelations' – to be limited in every particular by revelation, by the Lord Jesus Christ: 'When I am weak, then I am strong.'

We have to do here with an order that can be forgotten or infringed only to the detriment of a real knowledge of the truth of the Christian religion. If ever the demonstrative power for this truth is ascribed to the religious self-consciousness as such, it is to the dishonour of God and the eternal perdition of souls. Nothing, however, has done and can do more harm to the church outwardly as well, in its debate with the non-Christian religions, than when it thinks it has to evade the apostolic injunction that grace is sufficient for us. The place where we then try to look is hazy, and the reed that we then want to lean upon will slip through our hands. For then we are placing ourselves on the same ground as the other religions that we want to refute and overcome. They too all appeal to this or that truth inherent in themselves. They too would like to triumph by the power of the religious self-consciousness and have sometimes done so in an astonishing way over wide areas. Christianity can take part in this struggle. There is no doubt that it does not lack the necessary equipment and can stand honourably alongside the other religions. But let us not forget: it has then renounced its very birthright, the unique power accruing to it as the religion of revelation. That power dwells only in weakness. That power would in fact be effective, and with it the very thing by which Christianity now believes it can be effective, namely, the power given to it by grace in the midst of its weakness that is also the power of its religious self-confidence – both would in fact be effective only if Christianity had first humbled itself instead of exalting itself.

The difficulty that Christianity has brought upon itself in its debate with the other religions by neglecting this order can be seen to have developed in three historical stages.

1. It was no doubt least apparent in the time of the early church before Constantine. At that time Christianity, as *religio illicita*, as *ecclesia pressa*,[3] had the great advantage of being pushed mechanically, as it were, close to the apostolic situation, that is, the apostolic weakness. The adherents of the Christian religion could not, at any rate, take much credit externally for their status, politically, socially, or culturally. They found themselves alone with their faith over against a hopelessly superior external force. They were fighting at an abandoned outpost. The angel of Satan really did seem to harass them too, to keep them from being too elated by the abundance of revelations. They seemed to be almost automatically directed to boast in fact only of this their weakness, that is, to

let grace be sufficient for them. But the superior external force of the pagan world of late antiquity that was ranged against them was in the end a colossus with feet of clay – as the Apologists, the early Church Fathers, and certainly all the more insightful leaders of the church of that day recognized perfectly well, despite all the pressure of persecution. Christian doctrine and practice had all the necessary qualities to commend itself over against this paganism as the more profound, the more universal, the more serious religion. It became a temptation not only to affirm Jesus Christ against, or for, the sinful people of pagan religiosity, as the holy books of the church, the Old and New Testaments, demanded. Rather, the temptation was, in addition (as happened quite quickly along a fairly broad front), to play off the Christian religion as the better one over against the religions of the pagans, to present the Christian possession as the alternative to pagan poverty – a possession that can easily be demonstrated in many, if not all, spheres of spiritual life. In reading the apologetics of, say, the second and third centuries, one cannot entirely avoid the uncomfortable impression that what we have here is, to a great extent – as though the persecuted had to compensate in the spiritual sphere for the external pressure brought against them – a kind of not very happy, rather self-righteous, and at any rate imprudent bragging about all sorts of advantages, undeniable in themselves but hardly decisive, which Christianity possesses over against the world of pagan religion. In these early Christian self-recommendations a remarkably minuscule part is played by the fact that grace is the truth of Christianity; that the Christian, like Abraham, is the godless one who has been justified, the publican in the temple, the prodigal son, the poor Lazarus, the guilty thief crucified with Jesus Christ. Rather, we see here one way of salvation competing – without doubt successfully – with others, one wisdom with others, one morality with others, a higher humanity, consummated and transfigured by the cross of Christ, competing with a decadent, demoralized humanity rightly grown weary of its old ideals. How strange that a man like Tertullian saw the danger that threatened here and at the same time did not see it at all but rather helped to increase it! The fact that grace, that Jesus Christ, is the truth of Christianity did not remain wholly concealed in the teaching and proclamation of the church. And to the extent that this was recognized, did not the fact of Christianity as the special religion of grace and redemption also easily appear to be its ultimate and highest advantage, yet one whose meaning and persuasive power was taken away because the church did not in fact allow grace to be sufficient for it? And to the degree that here, materially and formally, that which was centrally and authentically Christian was abandoned or even reversed, there occurred conversely all kinds of material and formal accommodations to the world, which they thought they could overcome at least spiritually. Against the force of syncretism, which was so characteristic of that waning spiritual world, only the force of spiritual poverty and the power of revelation within it could have prevailed. So long as this force remained or reappeared periodically on the scene, the truth of Christianity spoke and shone forth. So long as the early church was great, it was great by means of this force. If only the early church had not trusted all too much in other forces and thereby weakened itself and prepared the way for further weakenings!

2. The external pressure under which the church originally stood, and along with it the external similarity with the original apostolic situation, a certain

compulsion continually to reflect upon and to return to what was ultimate and authentic – all this came to an end in the developments after Constantine and in the whole period governed by the idea of the *corpus christianum*.[4] Certainly one can and must also understand this idea of the unity of church and empire as a most promising *offer* made to Christianity at this time. One must immediately add, however, that it proved at that time to be thoroughly unready for this offer, unable to cope with the temptations bound up with this offer. Already the early church had reflected upon and returned more to its intellectual than to its spiritual superiority over against the pagan environment, had presumed more upon its monotheism, its morality, and its mystery than upon the grace of Jesus Christ. So now, as the recognized church of the empire, in open alliance with the higher and lower political factors, the church found it possible to seek its greatness in the fact that it was increasingly becoming a second world power. It could pursue its ambition – under the heading, of course, of honouring God – by seeking to become not just the second but the first and true world power. Where was the knowledge of grace as the truth of Christianity in the days of the investiture controversy and the crusades, in the world of the Gothic? To what extent was it the real concern in the great reform movement of Cluny and in monasticism generally? To what extent could pagans and Jews encounter in the church of the Middle Ages a truly different power, one new and unknown to them – not the power that men have always been in a position to demonstrate over against other men, but rather the power of God that humbles and thus blesses all men, the power of the gospel? To what extent did the church have something really original with which to oppose the Islam that was besieging it in the east and south? To what extent could even the Christian opponents of the church – the imperial and national movements, for example, or even the heretical sects – deduce from the actions and attitude of the church that it was really a matter of God's and not the church's own glory? They could obviously do so all the less as the spiritual estrangement of the church from its own centre, which went hand in hand with the inner secularization that had already started in antiquity, advanced further and further in this period. Christianity now formed itself into a specific universal intellectual-moral-aesthetic worldly configuration, whose possible and necessary complement was the formation of all kinds of special national Christianities, each with its own particular national-religious self-consciousness. To what extent was this worldly configuration, in itself or in its individual varieties, a witness to the truth of Christianity? It certainly *was* a witness to a strange and rich religious self-consciousness, namely, a witness to the glory of Western man, brought up and educated, and even animated and influenced, by the church as the (all too legitimate!) heir of ancient culture. It was able to be a witness to the superior and victorious truth of Christianity, however, only to the extent that, secretly and ultimately, it had also to do with the grace of Jesus Christ. And precisely in this decisive respect the church, so actively zealous and concerned in other respects, exercised too little vigilance and loyalty. If the witness to grace did not simply perish but rather proved its quiet power, if revelation shone even in this world in the spiritual poverty of those who believed in it as it is meant to be believed, then this happened in the church against the church, that is to say, against the prevailing tendency in the church, against the proud and yet so treacherous idea of the *corpus christianum*.

Along the very path where it sought its strength, the church, again in this age, did all too much that was bound to weaken it at the critical point.

3. So-called modernity, which took its start with the Renaissance, though not without preparation in the tendencies of the later Middle Ages, is characterized with respect to Christianity by the dissolution of that unity of empire and church. Western humanity has come of age, or thinks it has.[5] It can now dispense with its teacher – and that is indeed what official Christianity had felt itself to be and how it had behaved. Man discovers himself to be the universal and, even if he does not so readily abandon his reverence for the teacher, now feels himself capable of going his own way with his head held high. Politics, the sciences, society, and the arts, grateful for all they have received but determined upon a profane objectivity, all dare to stand on their own feet once again. The flood waters have subsided, and behold! – not much more than a bit of monotheism, morality, and mystery appears to remain after the thousand-year alleged dominion of Christianity. Western humanity appears on the whole to have found nothing more than that in the church or connected with the church, and nothing more seems to bind it to the church – that's the happy discovery it now makes. Nor do the pagans surrounding the little peninsula of Europe and its overseas colonies, or the Jews continuing tenaciously to exist in the midst of Christendom, appear to have heard anything more than that through the mouth of the church – at least not in a way that made an impression. Evidently the Christian church, despite such favourable conditions in the Middle Ages, did not know how to make any more of an impression on the world's consciousness than that of a 'religious society'. In trying under those favourable conditions to prevail and to bind, it did not in fact prevail or bind at all, as is now becoming evident in the increasing secularization of the entire culture. It is forced once again, as in ancient times, on to the defensive. For the time being, to be sure, there is no talk of outward oppression and persecution. What reason could there be for that? One fought against the church right into the nineteenth century when it was a matter of emancipation from its medieval claims. But the church is granted its freedom so long as it agrees on its part to observe a certain restraint and tolerance. For the time being, there is no longer any question of its being so dangerous that it would need to be persecuted on principle, as the dying ancient empire had done in full awareness of the situation. Rather, for some centuries the only question to arise is the possibility that the church, that Christianity, confined to its proper place in service to the new secular splendour of Western man, might be an important and, with suitable oversight, a useful force for education and order, and as such might be put to good use. And the non-Christian religions, too, stand facing the new Christianity, to the extent that they come into contact with it, on the same terms as the intra-Christian secularism, quite content with a bit of restraint and tolerance, and maintaining on their part a mild indifference. Things could indeed get dangerous again for modern secularism and the non-Christian religions should the truth of Christianity, the grace of Jesus Christ in its radical critical power, ever again find expression. It is telling that the only case in which the church actually ever came under attack in modernity, the persecutions that early Protestantism had to endure for a time in a number of lands, had to do precisely with the fact that this truth again found expression. But that was long ago. Once the medieval dream was over,

3. The True Religion

Protestantism too had first of all to adapt itself, and knew it had to do so, to the way of existence as a religious society that was ultimately unnecessary and unthreatening to modern man. And on the whole, the new Christian church did not at first even think of returning to the false direction initiated in ancient times and of recovering what had been openly omitted in the Middle Ages. In the reconsideration of itself and its possibilities imposed upon it in the new situation, it again failed to attain to that weakness by which alone it could be strong in all times. Instead, it basically affirmed the new situation inwardly in the same way it had previously affirmed the old one: it acknowledged in principle the modern man who so firmly relies on himself, and then wondered how Christianity might best commend itself to that man. It accepted the auxiliary role which had been assigned to it and sought to make itself indispensable in that role, that is, to demonstrate and make visible that the truth of the Christian religion, which even in the new age is good and useful to hear and to believe, consists in this: the rightly understood doctrine of Jesus Christ and its corresponding way of life have the secret power to make man inwardly capable of striving for and attaining the very goals and purposes that he has independently chosen. In pursuing this new self-commendation, Christianity – along the related lines of Jesuitism, pietism, and the Enlightenment – became secular-*anthropo*logical in the same way that in the Middle Ages it had been secular-*theo*logical. And precisely in pursuing this new self-commendation, it arrived at the discovery, among others, of the general concept 'religion', whose theological history we have briefly recalled. Everything now depended, within this general concept that was likewise accepted by the non-Christian world, on illuminating and presenting in a reliable way the particular 'essence of Christianity', and doing so on the same human plane and from the same points of view, on a par with the same arguments as those with which they thought they could dispense – namely, in the realm of human and humanly comprehensible advantages and disadvantages, strengths and weaknesses, probabilities and improbabilities, hopes and fears. In a way not dissimilar to the situation in the Roman Empire – but without the corrective of outward oppression – Christianity was now compared with its various competitors as the better foundation for world view and morality, as better able to satisfy ultimate needs, as the better actualization of the highest ideals of modern man. In this of all times, and under these of all circumstances, and carried out by the Jesuits and the Protestant Pietists of all people – there now occurred a comprehensive revival of the *missionary* task of the Christian church, and as a result a new confrontation of Christianity with the extra-Christian religions. It was unavoidable that the mission and the confrontation had at first to suffer grievously because the missionary church itself generally sought its strength otherwise than in the place where it could have been found. Likewise the debate about whether the aim of the mission should be to represent a European–American Christianity or to found an autochthonous African and Asian Christianity could not remove the hidden problem that either way it was still a matter of the 'glory' of one Christianity or the other in its relation to the needs and postulates of man. Nevertheless, in this third period in the Christian West as well, and in the mission fields, the truth of Christianity, the grace of Jesus Christ in the spiritual poverty of those who believed in him even in this period did not fail to speak, to shine forth, and to assert itself. But in this period

97

as well it had to do so in contradiction to the dominant trends and tendencies in church history. So long as these tendencies and trends were dominant and determined the situation, Christianity could only deliver its truth to the continually changing shape of modern man in such a way that it was tossed back and forth from one unclean hand to the other, appearing as a human truth – now absolutistic and authoritarian, now individual and Romantic, now liberal, now national or even racial – but never as the divine truth that judges and blesses, as it has claimed to be again and again, in accordance with the ancient documents of Christianity, which strangely enough have never been entirely silent. At this third stage of their history Christianity and the church have experienced many victories – more than one would have dreamed of at the highpoint of this period in the eighteenth century. No one should be deceived, however, about the fact that they were Pyrrhic victories. And at least as many defeats were suffered along the same road, and they were more indicative of the actual state of affairs. If it is the case that modern secularism for its part is still far from the end of its ways and possibilities, and that the powers of the pagan religions are still far from exhausted, then it could become an ever more burning question whether Christianity, from the point of view of its very existence, of its validity and task in the world, does not have good reason to tackle its *own* secularism and paganism, but that means – for everything else is secular and pagan – to set its hope wholly upon grace.

We must not allow ourselves to be confused by the fact that a history of Christianity can only be written as a history of this problem that it creates for itself. It is a history that remains wholly behind the history that has taken place between Yahweh and his people, between Jesus and his apostles. It is a history whose origin, meaning, and goal – namely, the fact that the Christian is strong only in his weakness, that he truly allows grace to be sufficient for him – is, strictly speaking, nowhere directly visible. Not even in the history of the Reformation! What is visible historically is the attempt undertaken by the Christian, in ever-changing ways, to regard and to validate his religion as a proper and holy work in itself – except for the fact that from time to time he finds himself harassed, hampered, and impeded by Holy Scripture, which doesn't allow him to do this, and which seems to want to subject even this Christian religion of his to criticism – and except for the fact that he obviously can't get rid of the memory that he also cannot do without the grace of God precisely when it comes to the work of his religion and therefore stands under God's judgment. This is just the place where Reformation history ought especially to be recalled; but it should also be recognized precisely in light of Reformation history that the periods before and after it were not simply without this memory. Nevertheless: the history of Christianity as a whole shows a current running directly against this memory. It would be biased to fail to recognize this fact and so to claim that the history of Christianity, in contrast to that of the other religions, were the history of one part of humanity which, in contrast to others, did in fact stand out as one that had lived by grace through grace. Strictly speaking, that becomes visible nowhere in the whole Christian field. Rather, what does become visible to us is, to begin with at any rate, a part of humanity that contradicts the grace, and thereby the revelation, of God no less because it claims them to be its special and most holy possessions, and because its religion is to this extent the religion of revelation. Contradiction is contradiction. The fact that it takes place here, with regard to the religion of revelation itself, can be denied even less than elsewhere, where one might at least be able to claim in mitigation that the contradiction takes place only in effect but not in direct opposition to revelation; whereas here, in the history of Christianity, just because it is the religion of revelation, one sins, as it were, with impunity. Sins! For to contradict grace is faithlessness, and faithlessness is sin, even the very epitome of sin. It is already implicit in the fact that we can really speak about the truth of the Christian religion in no other way than in the context of the doctrine of *iustificatio impii*.[6] The very sea of naive and sophistical contradiction raised against the proposition that the Christian religion also comes under the rule that 'religion is faithlessness' – the whole history of the church is a history of this contradiction – is the best evidence for how true and right this proposition really is. We will certainly no more be able to get free of this contradiction than to leap over our own shadow.

> Nor can we expect that in a fourth, fifth, or sixth stage the history of Christianity will be anything else but a history of that problem which Christianity creates for itself. May it also in the future not be without reformations, that is, appeals of warning and promise from Holy Scripture! Before the end of all things we cannot expect that the Christian, notwithstanding all his scruples to the contrary, will not again and again prove himself to be an enemy of grace.

But in spite of this contradiction, and therefore in spite of our own existence, we can and must discern that precisely we ourselves, together with the contradiction of grace on our part, stand under the far more powerful contradiction of grace itself. We can and must – in faith, of course! Faith means relying, in the knowledge of our own sin, upon the righteousness of God that eternally makes amends for our own sin; and so concretely it means holding on, in the knowledge of one's own contradiction of grace, to the grace of God that eternally contradicts our contradiction. In *this* knowledge of grace – in the knowledge that it is the justification of the godless, that grace is also and especially for the enemies of grace – the Christian faith performs its knowledge of the truth of the Christian religion. There can therefore be no more question of any immanent rightness or holiness of this particular religion being the ground and content of its truth than there can be of any other religion claiming to be the true religion by virtue of its immanent advantages. Rather, it is precisely the *surrender*, so unavoidable for the Christian faith, of this claim; it is precisely the *confession*, so inevitable for the Christian, that he is a sinner even in his best Christian actions – this is not the ground, of course, but surely the *symptom* of the truth of the Christian religion. For this surrender, this confession can indicate that the Christian church is the place where human beings are confronted with God's revelation and grace, where they live by grace through grace. If this were not so, how could they have faith? And if they did not have faith, how could they be capable of this surrender and this confession?

> The passage in Gen. 32:22f. about Jacob's struggle at the Jabbok can shed some light at this point. We are told that this Jacob, who is doubtless already one chosen and called by God, wrestled with God until the break of day, and that God – note well! – did *not* overcome him. Observed intrinsically, he is and remains, therefore, an enemy of grace. This is indicated also by the new name 'Israel' that he subsequently receives: 'You have striven with God and with men, and have prevailed' – a great, but in fact shattering distinction, which may well remind us of the history of the religion of the people whose ancestor this Jacob was. But the meaning and point of this story is not the distinction of Jacob by this name, which in fact carried out the judgment. Rather, its meaning and point is (1) that in the course of this struggle Jacob's hip was touched by God and dislocated, so that even though he was not overcome by God he becomes and remains one *weakened* by God; (2) that Jacob, in wrestling with God, will *not let go* of God because he wishes to be blessed by him; (3) that God in fact *blesses* him, his dogged opponent; and (4) that Jacob calls the place of this struggle Peniel: 'For I have seen *God face to face*, and yet my life is preserved.'
>
> The place where the truth of the Christian religion is known will also have to be such a Peniel; and such a Peniel can only be where man stands wholly and completely opposed to God, and in this very resistance against God becomes one marked by God, and precisely as such cannot make any other request than this, 'I will not let you go, unless you bless me', and precisely in this prayer he is heard and is therefore blessed, and precisely as one so blessed he sees God's face and in it knows the truth.

When we designate the victorious *grace* of God as the mystery of the truth of the Christian religion, we must once again expressly emphasize that we mean something more than that in its *Reformation* form, at any rate, Christianity intends with special emphasis to be the religion of free grace, that is, a religion whose doctrine and life is concentrated specifically on the reality designated by the concept 'grace'. Establishing the truth of the Christian religion by grace is really not a matter of the immanent truth of any particular *religion* of grace as such but rather of the reality of grace *itself*, through which one religion is accepted and set apart from the others as the true one. This does not happen because it is a religion of grace, nor even because it is so perhaps in an especially emphatic and consistent way. Rather, it is the other way around: because this happens, the religion will be a religion of grace in an especially emphatic and consistent way. Indeed, the historical face of a religion of grace, even a consistent one, is no different in its decisive features from that of other religions. In its immanent content it too is thoroughly involved in that contradiction of grace; it may even – and here we really cannot hope to save Protestantism – take on the character of an especially emphatic rebellion against grace. Even the religion of grace can be justified and made into the true religion only by grace itself and never by its own devices. Certainly its election and truth will also manifest themselves in the fact that it is a religion of grace and that it understands and shapes itself accordingly in ever more consistent ways. Certainly that symptom of surrendering every human claim will not fail to appear, nor the confession that we contradict God again and again. We cannot possibly omit the fact that in our contradicting we know ourselves to be cast completely upon the very one whom we contradict, and in our pleading to be pushed towards him – the one who contradicts us in a completely different way. And we cannot omit the praise of his blessing, of which we are so unworthy. It will be in this very encounter with God, whose place we may then call Peniel, or perhaps Protestant Reformed Christianity, that God's face is revealed, and thus Peniel, or Protestant Reformed Christianity, becomes the true religion. We will not then forget, however, that it is not those symptoms and therefore not these places named by us that establish the true religion, but rather the truth itself is the ground of those symptoms and has set these places apart so that we might call them by these names – but without being bound to these particular symptoms and these particular places. If we are not to deceive ourselves concerning the truth of the Christian religion when we regard these symptoms, however distinct, or these places, however distinguished, then the truth itself will always be required.

We may surely call it an almost providential occurrence that the most exact, comprehensive, and plausible 'pagan' parallel to Christianity, as far as I can see, is a form of religion in the Far East that parallels not so much Roman or Greek Catholicism but rather of all things the Christianity of the *Reformation*, and therefore confronts Christianity with the question of its truth precisely in its form as a consistent religion of *grace*. It concerns two interrelated forms of Buddhism in Japan in the twelfth and thirteenth centuries (thus during the lifetimes of Francis of Assisi, Thomas Aquinas, and Dante): the *Yodo-Shin* ('Sect of the Pure Land', founded by Genku-Honen) and the *Yodo-Shin-Shu* ('True Sect of the Pure Land', founded by Genku's disciple Shinran).[7]

The point of departure of these movements, which formed a turning point in Japanese religious history, was Genku's view that the earlier forms of Japanese Buddhism – particularly those of the Zen sects that flourished in the twelfth century, with their demand for a redemption through man's own powers, specifically by striving after a higher morality, a mystical absorption and contemplative knowledge as the 'path of holiness' – were, to be sure, venerable and correct in themselves, but for the great mass of the people quite simply too difficult and hence impracticable. In its place Genku wanted to establish a considerably easier method of salvation. The deity that he shifted to the centre for this purpose was the 'Amida-Buddha', proclaimed since the seventh century in China – perhaps not without connection to the Nestorian[8] mission – and since the eighth century also in Japan, called 'Infinite Light' or 'Infinite Life' and, at least in popular belief, thought also to be the supreme personal God. This Amida, so it is taught, is creator and lord of a paradise, a 'Pure Land [*yodo*] in the west'. To be reborn there after death, in order to reach Nirvana from there, is the task of human life. 'There we will sit in blessedness crossed-legged on lotus flowers, and in the contemplation of Amida gradually develop to full maturity of knowledge, in order at last to enter Nirvana' (Florenz, p. 387). But how do we arrive at this rebirth? Not by our own power, answers Genku in sharp contrast to the other Buddhist sects. And now he takes up a crucial text, adopted from the Chinese Amida tradition and most emphatically called by him the 'original promise', containing a *vow* by the God Amida himself, according to which he himself, Amida, will not accept perfect enlightenment (Budda-hood) unless all living beings who with upright heart believe in him and implore him ten times with the wish for rebirth into his land might also participate in the fulfilment of this wish. Therefore, Genku teaches, we have to place our complete trust not in our own power but in that of this other, Amida. We have to fulfil the one condition that he has attached to the attainment of salvation: we must have *faith* in him, who is merciful to all, even sinners. We have to call upon his *name*, and by doing so all his good works and meritorious acts flow into our mouth and become our own possession, so that our merit becomes what Amida's merit is, and there is no longer any difference between him and us. One has to perform this invocation as often as possible. Especially at the decisive moment of death one has to be certain in invoking this name that Amida will not reject even the greatest sinners but will assign them at least a small corner in that paradise which is the forecourt of Nirvana. Those who have performed the invocation of Amida while entertaining secret doubts will be shut up for five hundred years in the cup of a lotus blossom that is likewise found in a small corner of paradise. And in a perfectly sensible way, for those who were unable to depend wholly on faith and thus on the power of this invocation but who wanted instead to rely also on the accomplishment of so-called good works and religious practices, there has been provided in the farthest west a place full of heavenly enjoyments, singing, dancing, and playing as a provisional accommodation, until they are permitted to leave this purgatory, equipped especially for their education, and enter the fields of supreme blessedness.

This particular doctrine of Genku and the Yodo-Shin was systematically developed in both its doctrinal and practical aspects by Shinran, the founder of Yodo-Shin-Shu, and made a matter of basic principle. Here too everything rests upon that original promise of the merciful redeemer Amida and upon faith in him. But while Genku still recognized the veneration of other Buddhas alongside Amida, such a practice is now expressly forbidden. Even Gautama Buddha now fades completely into the background as the mere proclaimer of the Amida doctrine. Meritorious good works, whose possibility Genku had not completely denied, are entirely absent in Shinran. Rather, everything now depends simply on the faith of the heart. For we are too deeply mired in carnal desires to be able through any kind of activity of our own to extricate ourselves from the corrupting cycle of life and death. The only human act remaining is thanksgiving for the redemption granted by Amida without any activity on the part of man. The hour of death now loses that critical character so emphasized in Yodo-Shu doctrine, just as the invocation of Amida now loses the last remnant of the character of an achievement or a magical act, likewise becoming entirely a sign of human gratitude. Genku's saying, 'Even sinners shall enter into life; how much more must it be possible for the good!' has been turned around in a significant way by Shinran: 'If even the good enter into life, how much more will it be so for the sinners!' The redemptive significance of faith in Amida depends neither on feeling, nor on joyfulness of heart, nor even on the strength of the desire for salvation. There are, to be sure, means for awakening and strengthening faith. One should, for example, make use of the opportunity to be schooled in the holy doctrine; one should reflect on its meaning; one should cultivate conversations about it with religiously-minded friends; one should speak the Amida prayer in a quiet voice; one should strengthen himself in the face of his utter sinfulness with the wonderful thought that on the basis of the original promise he is nevertheless not rejected. But one must also know that even faith in this original promise is finally itself a gift of the God. Yet this same faith is also now for everyone; it is a way readily open to women as well – an unheard-of innovation in the world of Buddhism. In view of all of this, it is understandable that Yodo-Shin-Shu knows of no petitionary prayer, no magical formulas or spells, no amulets, pilgrimages, penances, fasts, or other kinds of asceticism, and also therefore no monasticism. The sole cultic object in their rich temples is an image or statue of Amida. Their priests have no significance as mediators of salvation; their role is the instruction of the faithful and the cultivation of the ecclesiastical customs; they wear vestments only in the temple and are subject neither to special dietary laws nor even to celibacy. Great weight, on the other hand, is placed upon their activity in instruction, preaching, and popular literature for edification. The effect of the faith in Amida that is urged upon the laity is a moral way of life in the context of family, vocation, and the state. They should 'exercise self-discipline, live in harmony with others, preserve order, obey the laws of the state, and as good citizens promote the welfare of the state' (Florenz, p. 397). In contrast to the other Japanese sects, Yodo-Shin-Shu never allowed itself to be supported legally or financially by the government but has been from the outset a church entirely free of the state, preferring to be active in the large cities.

It is really no wonder that St Francis Xavier, who spent 1549–1551 as the first Christian missionary in Japan, thought he recognized quite simply the 'Lutheran heresy' in Yodo-Shin-Shu. The question thereby posed, however, has not only historical but very contemporary significance, for (according to Florenz, p. 398) even today nearly half the total population of Japan, or at least a good third of them, still belong to this church.

(Some have also been reminded in this context of Indian Bhakti piety. But this parallel, even if one grants it to be such, is far less convincing as compared to the Japanese case. Bhakti is the act of utter devotion and resignation in which one's will is placed wholly in the service of the other, and which can then even intensify into an act of heartfelt personal affection and love. The high or supreme God to whom Bhakti is offered may bear this or that name and character. It is

the feeling of love itself and as such that redeems man, that makes him a participant in the reciprocating love of God, but that also allows him on the earthly
plane to become sympathetic and merciful, unselfish, patient, and serene. We
are told of a certain neutralizing of all other means of salvation. We are told – in
a rather modest counterpart indeed to the Protestant doctrine of justification
– of a 'cat rule', according to which the soul can leave everything to God and
need make no effort itself because God leads it to salvation in the same way that
the cat carries her young – in contrast to a 'monkey rule', according to which
God's relationship to the soul is characterized by the image of a monkey, whose
young, in order to be carried by her, must keep holding on. Not only the very
uncertain position and role of the concept of God, but also the replacement
of the concept of faith by that of devotion and love, and in addition the utter
formlessness in all respects of this concept of love – all this shows that we find
ourselves here in a very different world from the Japanese religion of grace, and
totally different from Evangelical Christianity. It would be a very poor variety
of Evangelical Christianity indeed that could feel an attractive kinship to these
Bhakti religions!)

Only that 'Japanese Protestantism' of Genku and Shinran comes under
serious consideration in this context. When I described its existence as a providential occurrence, I meant that the striking parallelism with regard to the truth
of Christianity, far from causing us to be puzzled even for a moment, should
make us thankful for bringing home so very instructively the fact that the
Christian religion in its historical form as a mode of doctrine, life, and order *per
se* can never be the thing that contains the truth – not even if the form should
be that of Reformation Christianity. Its form, including its Reformation form,
obviously cannot be proved to be flawlessly original. Certainly no thoughtful
person would want to speak of an identity between Christian and Japanese
'Protestantism'. Two natural or historical forms, after all, do not tend to be
exactly the same. It is well to note, therefore, the following points. (1) The
starting point of the Yodo movement was, notoriously, the popular wish for an
easier and simpler path to salvation; but one could hardly say of Luther or
Calvin that they too began from exactly there. Accordingly, (2) among the ideas
of Yodo in parallel to those of the Reformation one fails to find any doctrine of
a law of Amida, or of his holiness, or his wrath; the goodness and mercy of this
God seems lacking in contrast, and as a result his redemption of man lacks
drama, lacks the character of a real solution to a real problem. It appears,
therefore, (3) that the Yodo antithesis to cultic and moral works-righteousness
also lacks that stress on a struggle for the honour of God against human
wilfulness and arrogance, which already in Paul himself, and in the Reformation
especially in Calvin, receives the real emphasis: Yodo appears to be based wholly
on a pastoral concern, which as such is taken to be obviously grounded beyond
question. (4) Yodo religion, along with the rest of Buddhism, thus stands or falls
with the inward power and validity of the passionate human desire for a
redemption through dissolution, for entry into Nirvana, to which the 'Pure
Land', to be reached by faith alone, is only the forecourt; the desire for Buddha-
hood, towards whose perfection even the God Amida is only on the way. In Yodo
religion this goal of human desire, and not Amida or faith in him, is the real
governing and determining force, to which Amida and faith in him and the 'Pure

3. The True Religion

Land', to which faith forms the entrance, are related only as means to the end. So, viewed at close range, there is no lack of notable immanent differences between the Japanese and the Christian 'Protestantism'. But the decisive point cannot be made by demonstrating these differences – which, viewed at still closer range, could no doubt be increased and deepened. Yodo religion can be compared with certainty and without violence only to a somewhat primitively understood Christian Protestantism, which has indeed existed in countless minds from the sixteenth century until today as the true Protestantism, or to a certain self-conception and self-presentation of Lutheranism in particular that is a far cry from Luther's own. One thinks instinctively of Pharaoh's magicians in Exodus 7, who were at least able to perform the miracles of Aaron, who after all was Moses' brother, well enough to give Pharaoh cause to harden his heart. With so many points of correspondence, even those differences might perhaps eventually wither away in a further immanent development of Yodo religion into a yet purer form – prompted (who knows?) by contact with Christianity! – thereby achieving after all an increasingly perfect likeness to Christian Protestantism, that is, to the purest form of Christianity as a religion of grace. But even if we do not take this possibility into account, we should still have every reason to see in these differences symptoms, but no more than symptoms, of the real difference between the true and the false religion. These symptoms, as such, have no decisive or really distinguishing power; they are not in themselves truth as opposed to falsehood but would have to receive the seal of truth from elsewhere. They are symptoms that could in principle be lacking – we must reckon with this theoretical possibility – without our therefore being allowed to doubt in the slightest the difference between truth and falsehood. The Protestant Christian religion of grace is not the true religion because it is a religion of grace. If it were, then the same might justifiably be said of the Yodo religion, whatever one might think about those differences; and with a somewhat blunted sensibility one could say it of Bhakti religion as well, and in that case why could the same not immediately be said also of a series of other religions for whom grace, under all kinds of labels and in all kind of contexts, is a not wholly alien quantity? Only one thing is really decisive concerning truth and falsehood. And the existence of Yodo religion is to be called providential because it makes clear with relatively great urgency that among the religions only one thing is decisive concerning truth and falsehood. That one thing is *the name Jesus Christ*. It might be methodologically advisable, in view of the Yodo religion but in principle in view of all the other religions as well, to consider first of all solely this difference and to put aside for the time being everything else that we think we know by way of differences: not only, for example, in the careful consideration of the developmental possibilities of pagan religions, which might one day overtake our doctrinal differentiations, but also in the clear insight that the truth of the Christian religion is in fact summed up in the name Jesus Christ and in nothing else. It is really summed up in the whole formal simplicity of this name as the essence of the reality of divine revelation, which all by itself constitutes the truth of our religion! Not, therefore, in its more or less distinctive structure as a religion of grace, nor in the Reformation doctrines of original sin, of vicarious satisfaction, of justification by faith alone, of the gift of the Holy Spirit, and of thanksgiving. All of this the pagans, to all appearances, can teach, and in their own way even live and express ecclesially, without thereby being any less pagans – poor, utterly lost pagans. Our knowledge, and the life of ourselves and our church, which accords with it tolerably well, distinguish us from them only to the extent that they are at best symptoms of that grace and truth which is Jesus Christ alone, and which therefore for us is the name Jesus Christ – only to the extent that they are utterly conditioned by this name and no other, and thus utterly bound to him, determined by him in content, directed towards him, and tested and confirmed by him. Christian Protestantism is the true religion to the extent that the Reformation was a reminder of the grace and truth summed up in this name, and that precisely this reminder is effective within it. In this reminder, which was more a being-reminded, Protestantism formed itself and was formed – and along with it, at least partially, the rest of Christianity as well – into what we now call its essence as an explicit religion of grace. This being-reminded led to the doctrines of justification and predestination, the evangelical doctrine of the church, of the sacraments, of the Christian life, and the other particulars that might distinguish it in this orientation in a more or less distinct way. As symptoms, predicates of the subject Jesus Christ – now, in retrospect, we may also speak seriously about them – these symptoms also certainly did receive, did have, and do have the power of truth: the power of *confessing* and *witnessing* to the truth. How could they not be required, and also well suited, to proclaim the name Jesus Christ and with it the truth of the Christian religion? And now: in this symptomatic power of confessing and witnessing, the not inconsiderable differences between the Christian and all non-Christian religions of grace may also become serious and important. For we may have good grounds for the conviction that even in view of their common structure there is in fact no possibility of confusing them with one another, that even in the future there will never in fact be a true parallelism, let alone a congruence, between the doctrine and life of one of the Christian religions of grace and one of the non-Christian ones (however consistent it may be!); but rather, that some sort of symptomatic differences will remain visible here and there from which it will always be possible to identify clearly the authentic, the essential difference. This conviction, however, will be a well-grounded one only if it is founded exclusively on faith in the one and only Jesus Christ, because only from him can those relative differences have, and continue to receive, their relative light. It will therefore be possible to prove the authentic and essential difference of the Christian religion in comparison to the non-Christian religions, and thereby its character as the religion of truth in comparison to the religions of falsehood, only in the fact, the event, in which the church, instructed by Holy Scripture, never tires but always stays awake to hear, proclaim, and believe Jesus Christ and no other to be grace and truth; and that it pleases him according to his promise to acknowledge this service offered to him, and so, in the confessing and witnessing of the church, to be his own confessor and witness. It is just here, in fact, that the church must be weak in order to be strong.

That there is a true religion is an event in the act of God's grace in Jesus Christ. More precisely: in the outpouring of the Holy Spirit. More precisely still: in the existence of the church and the children of God. If the church of God and the children of God exist, then there is true religion in the midst of the world of human religion – in other words, a knowledge and worship of God and a corresponding human activity, of which it cannot only be said that they are perverse, an attempt born of falsehood and wrong with unsuitable means; but rather one of which it is said that they (in their perversity) do in fact achieve their goal, that here (despite the falsehood and wrong that happens here too, and despite the unsuitability of the means applied here too) God is really known and worshipped, and the activity of man reconciled with God really takes place. The church and the children of God, and thus the bearers of the true religion, live by the *grace of God*, meaning that their knowledge of God, their worship of God, their service of God in doctrine, worship, and life is determined by their discernment of the free goodness of God, which anticipates all human thought, will, and action and corrects all human perversity, leaving man no response except faith and gratitude – yet even this is not his own work but the gift of God's grace – but which under no circumstances is ever denied to the man who is faithful and thankful. By living according to this order, the church and the children of God live by God's grace. But doing so is not the basis of their existence as church and children of God, nor is it what makes their religion the true religion. As far as this activity as such is concerned, they do not raise themselves to any significant degree above the level of religious history generally, nor do they escape the divine accusation of idolatry and works-righteousness. In the first place, their life by grace appears, historically at least, to be little more than an occasional scruple about the fulfilment of the law of all religion, which operates both beyond and also within their own sphere. If only the thought, will, and action of Christians as those who live by grace were really the criterion of their existence as church and children of God – with what boldness this existence of theirs and the truth of their religion could then be affirmed! But in the second place, one cannot affirm it on the basis of this criterion, because an ostensible, and sometimes a most impressive ostensible life by grace – i.e., the phenomenon of a religion of grace – is not entirely unknown in other areas of religious history as well. Measured by biblical standards, however, we do not therefore have cause to speak of church and children of God, of the existence of true religion, in these areas. Something quite different is decisive for the existence of the church and the children of God and for the truth of their religion – decisive thus also with regard to their living by grace, which is so problematic in itself – namely, that they live *though the grace of God* by his grace. That is what makes them what they are, makes their religion true, raises them above the level of religious history in general. Through the grace of God: but that means through the reality of that by which they ostensibly, and yet so problematically, live; through the reality by which man ostensibly and very problematically can also live if need be in other areas of religious history. Through the reality: in other words, through the fact that God, beyond all human accounting, beyond that which men can think, will, and do in the field of their religion, even if it is a religion of grace, really does act towards them as the gracious God that he is, apart from their merit or their worthiness; really does anticipate their thought, will, and action in his free goodness, really does awaken faith and gratitude in them, really never fails them. They are what they are, and their religion is the true religion, not by virtue of the fact that they acknowledge him as such and act accordingly, thus not by virtue of their religion of grace, but rather by virtue of the fact that God has accepted them in grace, thus by virtue of his mercy in spite of their ostensible and yet so problematic religion of grace, by virtue of the pleasure he takes in them, by virtue of the free choice whose only motive is this very pleasure, by virtue of his Holy Spirit, which he willed to pour out upon them. The fact that the church and the children of God live through his grace by his grace, thereby becoming the site and the bearers of the true religion, is something that we have only seen in its concrete significance, in its difference from any kind of higher principle of religion, which would fall under the same judgment as all human religion, when we are clear that 'through the grace of God' is utterly identical with '*through the name Jesus Christ*'. Because he, Jesus Christ, is the eternal Son of God and as such the eternal object of the divine pleasure; because he, as this eternal Son of God, became man; because in him man too has now become the object of divine pleasure, not by merit or worthiness but according to the grace that took on humanity in God's Son; because in this One the revelation of God among men, the reconciliation of man with God, has been consummated once and for all; because he gives the Holy Spirit – therefore and for these reasons, in this One there is a church of God and there are children of God. They are what they are, and they have the true religion, because he stands in their place, and therefore for his sake. They cannot for one moment wish to disregard him, with the notion and intention of being what they are by themselves or having the true religion by themselves. But even when they in fact disregard him – and this is just what they constantly do – this will of course cause them to become uncertain of their existence as church and children of God; but it can change nothing of the objective state of affairs that in him, in the name Jesus Christ – i.e., in the revelation and recon- ciliation that has taken place in him (nowhere else but really here!) – they are what they are, and are thereby bearers of the true religion. Therefore: through the grace of God there are men who live by his grace. Or stated concretely: through the name Jesus Christ there are men who have faith in this name. As long as this is the self-understanding of Christians and of the Christian religion, it can and must be said of it that it, and it alone, is the true religion.

This proposition, with its peculiar basis, must now be expounded and clarified under four specific perspectives.

1. The relationship between the name Jesus Christ and the Christian religion has to do first of all with an act of divine *creation*. This means that

its existence in its historical form and in its individual determinations is not an independent or self-grounded existence. The name Jesus Christ alone created the Christian religion, and without it it would never have existed. But this must be understood not only historically; it must immediately be understood in an ongoing and therefore present sense. The name Jesus Christ creates the Christian religion, and without it it would not exist. For even if we want to speak of the Christian religion to begin with simply as a reality, then we cannot be content to look back on the fact of its creation and thus its presence, but we must rather understand it, as we do our own existence and that of the world, as a reality that is to be created and was created, not only today but also yesterday and tomorrow, through the name Jesus Christ. Without the act of its creation through the name Jesus Christ, which like creation generally is to be understood as *creatio continua*,[9] and thus above all without its Creator, it has no reality. If we wanted to speak of the Christian religion apart from the name Jesus Christ, we would in fact be left with only two things: (1) the general human religious possibility, which of course belongs to the so-called Christians just as much as to all other men, but which as such might equally well be realized in some non-Christian religion as in the Christian – indeed, according to its essence as a general human possibility, it could definitely be realized only in some known or still unknown non-Christian religion – a merely empty possibility, by the way, and therefore not a reality! And (2) the ruins, in the process of rapid and complete disintegration, of a quasi-religious structure that was once called Christianity and maybe even was, but that now, with its vital root severed, does not even have the viability of a non-Christian religion, but can only disappear and be replaced by some other religion that is at least capable of existence. There is no particular need to prove that the Christian religion would never have entered into history at all and would therefore never have existed without the creative power of the name Jesus Christ, understood in the strictest sense. Without this name the men of that day would have existed as bearers of that general human possibility under the specific determinations under which it was a possibility for the men of that day. And no doubt there would then have existed a rather contentedly untroubled religious Hellenism of Jewish, oriental, and occidental provenance and colouring. Christianity as a missionary, cultic, theological, political, and moral entity, however, has been on the scene from the beginning in no other way than in an indissoluble bond to the name Jesus Christ. And we can learn precisely from the church history of recent centuries that the existence of the Christian religion has in fact been bound to this name and to the act of divine creation and preservation signified by it. Eliminate this name, and you will not only have maimed and weakened this religion so that it could at best continue to vegetate as a 'Christianity without Christ', but rather you will have taken away the ground of its existence, simply condemning it to a speedy demise, as has happened to other religions for other reasons. If even for a moment we were to disregard the name Jesus Christ, the Christian church would lose the substance by virtue of which it maintains its position as an entity of a special order in the state and in society, and over against them; Christian piety (regardless of whether it claims to be more a piety of head, heart, or deed) would lose the substance by virtue of which it is something distinctive alongside morality, art, and science; Christian theology would lose the substance by virtue of which it is not philosophy, not philology, not historical science but really sacred learning; Christian worship would lose its sacramental and sacrificial substance by virtue of which it is more than a solemn, half exuberant and half superficial game. The Christian religion would lose its substance, and thereby its right to live, and surely before long its capacity to live as well! The Christian religion is the predicate of the subject of the name Jesus Christ. Without it, it is not only something else but nothing at all, and it will be unable to hide this fact for long. It was and is and will be, by virtue of the act of creation signified by this name. Precisely by virtue of this act of creation, however, along with its being it simultaneously receives its truth. Because it was and is and will be through the name Jesus Christ, it was and is and will be the true religion: the knowledge of God, the worship of God, the service of God, in which man is not alone with himself in defiance of God, but rather walks before God in peace with God.

But beware: for the very reason that this name signifies nothing less than the act of creation and the Creator of the Christian religion, it is completely out of the question that we could append this name after the fact, as though we had it at our disposal, to our supposedly Christian doctrines as an explanatory or intensifying addendum or even as a critical reservation; or that we should invoke it after the fact like a magic power on the occasion of our supposedly Christian undertakings; or that we should append it after the fact to our supposedly Christian institutions as pretext and purpose, as a stained glass window is installed after the fact in an otherwise completed church. The name Jesus Christ is precisely not a mere *nomen* in the sense of the well-known medieval controversy[10] but rather the essence and source of all reality. Unless it stands in sovereign creative power at the beginning of the Christian religion and in the expressions of its life, whatever is asserted by us after the fact at its end or climax is not the name Jesus Christ at all but rather a hollow sound that will by no means transform our human nothingness into divine fullness. Fullness rather than nothingness is there and only there where the name Jesus Christ really is the beginning of all things as the Creator of our doctrine, our undertakings, and our institutions.

The best way to understand theoretically what is meant here is to understand the Christian religion, which is after all nothing other than the earthly and historical life of the church and the children of God, as an annexe to the human nature of Jesus Christ, remembering what is said of his existence in John 1:14: there was never such a thing as the man Jesus outside the eternal reality of the Son of God. There was, to be sure, within the fullness of human possibility, in the line from Abraham to the Virgin Mary, also this possibility, which then found its realization in the man Jesus. But it did not find this realization independently but rather by the power of the creative act in which the eternal Son of God took up precisely this human possibility into his reality, thereby *giving* it, in his own reality, that reality which it did not have previously or in itself, and which, even in receiving it, in no way had it outside of *his* reality. The human nature of Jesus Christ, so we are told, does not have its own hypostasis but has it only in the Logos.[11] Now the same is also true of the earthly and historical life of the church and the children of God, and therefore of the Christian religion. It is the life of the earthly body of Christ and his members, who are called out of mere shadowy possibility into reality by him, the Head, who has taken them to himself and assembled them into the earthly form of his heavenly body. Detached from him they could only fall back into that shadowy possibility, that is, into that non-being from which they proceeded. They live in him or they do not live at all. By living in him they share in the eternal truth of his own life. But they only have the choice of living by this sharing in his life or not at all. Their sharing in the life of the Son of God, however, as the heavenly Head also of his earthly body, is precisely the name Jesus Christ.

2. The relationship between the name Jesus Christ and the Christian religion has to do with an act of divine *election*. Because the Christian religion neither possessed, nor ever can possess, a reality of its own, and because, considered by itself, it reduces to merely one possibility among many others – for this reason it did not and does not have anything of its own to bring to the name Jesus Christ that would make it worthy of being his creation and as such the true religion. If it becomes reality, then it does so on the basis of free election, based on God's mercy and inconceivable good pleasure and on nothing else whatever. One will be able after the fact, of course, to explain the necessity of the origin of the Christian religion in view of the development of Judaism and the political, spiritual, and moral relationships of the Mediterranean lands in the time of the Roman Empire. But one will never be able by this approach to explain it or derive it in its reality. The only historical explanation and derivation worth considering seriously, the one from the history of the covenant made with Israel, can be compelling and plausible only if it is undertaken from the perspective of the fulfilment of the old covenant precisely in the name Jesus Christ, from the perspective of the revelation that took place, was acknowledged, and was believed – and therefore under the presupposition of this name. The fact that it pleased God to reveal himself in the name Jesus Christ at that particular time and place and in this particular way had its necessity in itself, not in whatever circumstances and conditions may have preceded this name. It is also due to election by God's free mercy and good pleasure, however, from that day on and right up to today, whenever Christian religion, by the power of Jesus Christ, is reality and not nothingness. Just as there is a *creatio* so too is there an *electio continua*,[12] which we would do better to describe as God's faithfulness and patience. The name Jesus

Christ is not bound mechanically, as though under an imposed constraint, to whatever seems to have reality and claims reality as Christianity – as a Christian doctrine or attitude or institution – supported by supposedly Christian people and supposedly Christian portions of the rest of mankind. Wherever this name is bound to it, it has bound itself, and the fact that it has done so will be due in every case to grace and not to human, not even to Christian, merit. For grace, and in this respect election – i.e., free grace – is, after all, also God's faithfulness and patience. It is election whenever the church is not just any religious society among so many others but rather the body of Christ, whenever it has not just aspirations but inspirations, whenever its relation to state and society is a relation of genuine opposition and in just this way genuine communion. Even the fact that it administers the word and the sacraments, that it possesses the scripture and the creeds, does not change in any way the fact that all of this is election, unmerited grace. It is election whenever its worship is not simply an oddly mixed variety of Jewish synagogue worship and the mystery cults of late antiquity but rather the worship of God in spirit and in truth. No tradition, however faithfully cultivated, and no contemporary religious consciousness, however lively, is able to prevent it from being just the former. If it is otherwise, if the supposedly spiritual is really spiritual, then it is only through the Holy Spirit, which blows where it wills, only on the basis of God's free, merciful turning towards us, and thus through election and not through some immanent aptitude for true spirituality. It is election whenever theology is not a science without an object, whenever it hears and expounds God's word not just supposedly and allegedly, thereby endeavouring to serve the purity of church doctrine. There is no method, no attitude, no orientation by means of which one might force theology to be something other than Rabbinic scriptural scholarship or Greek speculation. If it is something different, if it is genuine ecclesial science, then it is so at every step on the basis of election and not otherwise. We could say the same about Christian piety, Christian morality, Christian charity, Christian education, Christian politics. We have to remember in general that the weighty adjective 'Christian' – with which we expressly pronounce the name Jesus Christ – can therefore never be a grasping after our own possession but only our reaching out after the possession of God that is summed up in this name, and therefore an asking after our election, a request – that God not turn his countenance from us, that he might not weary of his unmerited faithfulness and patience. Where this adjective is really valid, there election has taken place. And it is precisely election that makes the Christian religion into the true religion. Note well: it is precisely election! It is therefore not the case that thinking of God's grace, which alone is decisive and bound to no human, not even Christian, possession, would mean a weakening of the certainty of Christian truth. Rather, with just *this* thought, however shattering its effect must be on all self-certainty regarding the truth, our eyes are opened to the basis of real certainty: the Christian religion is the true religion because it has pleased God, who alone can be judge in this matter, to affirm it in particular as the true religion. What is truth if not this divine Yes? And what is certainty of truth if not that certainty which is based only on this free judgment – free, but in its freedom, because it is the freedom of God, also wise and righteous?

From the perspective of election, we must also emphasize strongly that the relationship between the name Jesus Christ and the Christian religion is not reversible. Think of Ps. 100:3 in Luther's version:[13] 'Know ye that the LORD he is God: it is he that hath made us, and not we ourselves; we are his people, and the sheep of his pasture.' And John 15:16: 'Ye have not chosen me, but I have chosen you, and ordained you, that ye should go and bring forth fruit, and that your fruit should remain.' Both passages are directed especially to the religious community of the religion of revelation. The church and the children of God will again and again be tempted to assume themselves to be the ones doing the choosing in this relationship, to assume that their faith and their love, their creeds, their tradition, and their hope are its real substance, in comparison to which its founding on the name Jesus Christ may then suddenly look like a free bonus. One chooses it, no doubt, in utter earnest; however, by the very fact that one thinks that here he can and should choose, he shows that he no longer knows whose name it has to do with. We find the name Jesus Christ in this role of a king who is elected, and then re-elected again and again, yet finally just elected,[14] more or less throughout the theology, and likewise the piety and church life, of the eighteenth to the twentieth centuries. Clearly the Christian religion in these centuries thought that it could obtain its crucial nourishment from its own substance, that is, from Christian experience, morality, and world order as such. As a rule that did not mean, of course, that one wished to dispense with the name Jesus Christ or even to deny him the necessary love and respect. One certainly thought that the *beneficia Christi*[15] were to be seen also in the substance of the Christian religion itself. The individual radicals of this period – such as Reimarus in the eighteenth century, David Friedrich Strauss in the nineteenth, and Arthur Drews in the twentieth[16] – appeared even in the midst of liberal, not to mention conservative and pietistic, Protestantism as unwelcome rowdies in the midst of a fairly pious society. And they were treated accordingly by all sides. But the mixture of pity, anger, and palpable fear with which this happened nevertheless gave things away. As too did the pious and learned apologetic zeal – displayed again and again, first under this title and then under that, by all sides, and not least by the liberals – to secure, or to restore and re-establish, the traditional central role and place of honour to the name Jesus Christ in opposition to those radicals. If it had in fact retained or recovered that place, they might have saved themselves the effort: Luther and Calvin did not have to seek the fame of a 'christocentric' theology, which was the claim to fame, for example, of Schleiermacher and also of A. Ritschl and his disciples in the modern period, because the Reformers' theology was christocentric from the outset, without the singular attempt to call it so deliberately, and therefore without the need to become so. But how is theology, piety, or church life to become christocentric if it is not so from the outset? Precisely the efforts, the unhealthy zeal, the historical and systematic artistry they employed in the modern period in order to become christocentric testified loudly and clearly that they were not so from the outset and therefore could not become so now. They testified, namely, that they, just like those radicals, thought they had a choice in the matter at any rate, even though they chose differently. This notion of being able to choose vis-à-vis the name Jesus Christ was what most deeply undermined the credibility of the Jesuolatry[17] of Pietism and the movements of Awakening of that time. Indeed, one can say that precisely the positive attempts that were made on behalf of the name Jesus Christ at that time show most clearly the state of rebellion in which the church fundamentally found itself. For it was rebellion, even if pious rebellion, when people thought they could and should, from the standpoint of the safe haven of a religion that is in any event satisfying, say Yes to the name Jesus Christ, and thus choose it; it was rebellion when people were in a position to enter into a discussion of this matter in the first place. It was of course no accident that the theology of this very time, when and in so far as it concerned itself with Jesus Christ – with decidedly apologetic intent – took as the particular object of its endeavours an abstractly considered earthly and historical life of Jesus. Also forgotten, of course, was the very thing that was self-evident to the christology of the early church: that the human nature of Christ, to which they now so impulsively devoted themselves, was not only not an independent reality at all, but rather that, even as the mere possibility which was then realized in the eternal Son of God, it was the object of an externally unmerited and unforeseeable election. Whereas now, in a remarkable misunderstanding of what the New Testament says plainly enough, they assumed some sort of piety or morality or even demonic power of Jesus of Nazareth to be the thing that was known with greatest certainty and that should in all events be presupposed, while assuming that his so-called Messianic consciousness, on the other hand, was the problematic element, to be affirmed only cautiously and hesitantly with many reservations. They did not notice that by this line of christological reflection they ultimately portrayed only themselves, and themselves in their own perplexity: the great certainty in which they believed themselves to be Christians and in possession of Christian experiences and thoughts, representatives of the Christian position; and the great uncertainty in which they at long last decided for the affirmative with regard to the question of whether or not the name Jesus Christ is necessary. Already with this allocation of emphasis, with the fact that one could see *no* problem in the former but a *problem* in the latter, with the naïveté in which they affirmed their own Christianness in contrast to the Yes-No-Yes with which they also decided finally for Jesus Christ – here, and not just indirectly but quite directly, everything was already lost, the confession of the name Jesus Christ was already abandoned. And it was tragic how all the academic seriousness, all the sincerity and thoroughness, even all the heartfelt and profound piety that was doubtless devoted specifically to this Yes-No-Yes in the modern period was able only to make the damage more and more visible. It is therefore also surely no accident that the psychological structure of the theologians and churchmen of this time in particular (most pronounced around the turn from the nineteenth to the twentieth century) was to a great extent one of a marked humourlessness, weariness, and sadness, not to say depression. How

114

could it be otherwise when, despite the sterling quality of their subjective effort, they were fighting for such a lost cause?

Now someone could certainly object: Is not the confession of the name Jesus Christ truly a free decision of the human being and in fact, therefore, a choosing of this name? The answer must be, Of course! It is unambiguously presented in this way in passages such as Mt. 16:13f. and Jn 6:67f. One might also think here of Josh. 24:15f.: 'And if you be unwilling to serve Yahweh, choose this day whom you will serve, whether the gods your fathers served in the region beyond the River, or the gods of the Amorites in whose land you dwell; but as for me and my house, we will serve Yahweh.' In this particular passage we would certainly have to give due consideration to the difference between the 'choosing' among the Mesopotamian and the Canaanite gods, which always remains possible for the people, and that being-chosen by Yahweh, which Joshua already has behind him. Objectively, this is surely the situation: a choosing does indeed take place here; it is the kind of choosing, however, which man, as assuredly as it is his own choosing, can always look back on only as something that has already taken place. But in the actual act of such choosing, man does not stand before two or three possibilities, among which he might choose; rather, he chooses the one, the only, possibility given to him: he chooses his chosenness. The choosing of the name Jesus Christ is such a choosing. 'Lord, to whom should we go?'[18] Those who acknowledge the name Jesus Christ and thereby choose are choosing the only possibility given to them, namely, the one given to them by Jesus Christ himself – 'You have the words of eternal life.' They choose, but they choose their chosenness. There can be no question of their possessing some substance of Christian religion already available before this choosing, which might subsequently play a role as motive and criterion of their choosing the name Jesus Christ. Rather, their decision is nothing but the acknowledgment of a decision already made regarding them, and it will only be in this very decision already made regarding them that they will then behold the substance of their more or less substantial religion. This is their decision: the decision of obedience vis-à-vis the decision taken in the freedom of God is what is described by Holy Scripture as the decision of faith, and in particular faith in the name Jesus Christ. The Reformers and the older Protestantism surely knew what they were doing when in the same breath they called upon man to make this decision, and to that extent undoubtedly appealed to his freedom, and then always went on immediately to describe (with greater or lesser emphasis!) predestination – that is, the choice made in the eternal decree of God, the chosenness that took place and is known in Christ – as the authentic object and content of the decision of faith. In the decision of faith ordered and understood in this way, and in it alone, do we have to do in reality with the name Jesus Christ. Otherwise, even when it appears to have to do with this name and allegedly does, it is nevertheless a mere *nomen*,[19] which as such has no power and can then certainly never be powerfully affirmed. The power of affirming the name Jesus Christ is either its own power or it is no power. And only in the decision of faith ordered and understood in this way can the truth also come into view and become certainty. The truth illuminates, it convinces, it asserts itself, because that choice is fulfilled whose freedom and power is that of the name Jesus Christ itself, and of it alone. As such it becomes, and as such it makes itself, the truth of the Christian religion, whereas we, in alleged possession of an abstract Christian religion, will always look in vain for the truth of the name Jesus Christ and will also then strive in vain to become certain of the truth of the Christian religion.

3. The relationship between the name Jesus Christ and the Christian religion has to do with an act of divine *justification*, or the forgiveness of sin. We have already said that the Christian religion as such has no worthiness of its own that could equip it ahead of others to be the true religion. We must now say even more plainly that in itself and as such it is utterly unworthy of that status. If it is to be the true religion, it will be so through election, we have said; and we must now be more precise: it will be so by virtue of divine justification of sinners, by virtue of divine forgiveness of sin. The structure of this religion certainly does stand out from others (most sharply in its Protestant form), and we will have to understand and appreciate that too as the work of the name Jesus Christ. It does not, however, stand out from them in such a way that we might in some way evade the judgment made by God's revelation that all religion is idolatry and works-righteousness. On the contrary, that history determined by Christianity, on the whole and in particular, the history of the church and the life history of the individual child of God – also takes place under this sign. The closer one looks – rather, the more brightly the light of revelation from Holy Scripture falls upon it – the more evident it becomes. Both as a whole and in particular, it is in itself not a justified but rather a sinful history, sinful not only in its form but also at its human root, and no less so than can be said of the history of Buddhism or of Islam. The hands into which God has given himself in his revelation are thoroughly unclean, and in fact seriously unclean hands. If our knowledge of the truth of the Christian religion were conditioned by the life of an inherent purity of the church of God as its site, and of an inherent purity of the children of God as its bearers; if it remained hidden from us that both are pure (pure in their impurity!) for the sake of the word spoken to them – then our knowledge of the truth of the Christian religion would surely vanish. For if I am looking at the redeemedness of the redeemed, or even – making a still worse mistake – at my own redeemedness, not hearing the word by which the church and the children of God are pure in their impurity and redeemed in their utter unredeemedness, I might feel that the creation and election of this particular religion as the true religion (even if I should like to assert it for some reason) is finally just an arbitrary assertion, not at any rate confirmed by the facts.

Now there is indeed a fact that confirms this assertion powerfully and decisively, removing all arbitrariness and making it into an utterly necessary assertion. But in order to see this fact, we must first – and we will have to come back to this 'first' again and again – bracket completely the whole realm of 'facts' that we or any human observers are able to perceive and assess, because it is related to that realm as the sun to the earth. The fact that the sun now illumines not that part of the earth but this part means for the earth no less than this: that here it is day and there night – even though the earth is nevertheless the same earth here as there; even though here as there, from the earth's point of view, there is nothing that it would not have at its disposal in the day; even though, on the other hand, without the sun it would be just as veiled in eternal darkness here as it is there; even though the fact that it is nevertheless day in one part has nothing at all to do with the nature of this particular part of the earth as such. In just the same way the light of the righteousness and judgment of God falls on the world of human religion, on one part of this world, on the Christian religion, so that this particular religion is not in the night but in the day, not wrong but right religion, not false but true religion. Even though, regarded in itself, it is no less human religion and therefore faithlessness than all the other religions; even though there is nothing that we can demonstrate – neither in the root nor the crown of this particular tree, neither at the source nor the mouth of this particular stream, neither on the surface nor in the depths of this particular piece of humanity – that would make it suitable for the day of the righteousness and judgment of God. The reason why the Christian religion is the right and true religion, therefore, does not lie in any facts that it itself or its adherents might be able to demonstrate, but rather in the fact that confronts it along with all the other religions as the righteousness and judgment of *God*, identifying and singling it out specifically, it and not one of the other religions, as the right and true one. Note well: not an arbitrary whim, but rather the *righteousness* and the *judgment* of God is the decisive fact confronting them. What happens here is already fully in order, precisely because it is God's order that here becomes evident and takes effect – however surprising it may be from our point of view. What is enacted here is, of course, an acquittal that is completely inconceivable to us; but the acquittal is a judgment, and indeed a just one – although we have no insight into its motives. So we must not say, for example, that on the basis of that fact of God some other religion could just as well have been the right and true religion; rather, by recognizing and acknowledging the judgment pronounced in this fact of God, we must accept it as it is, without reckoning with the possibility that it might have been otherwise. But we would immediately deprive ourselves of the very unconditioned character of this knowledge if we did not allow it to be knowledge of the divine judgment in its entirety and thus knowledge of that fact of God – if instead, we tried to peer beyond that fact of God, wanting to take into account some sort of conditioning factors of the judgment in the character of the Christian religion as such. Looking in this way at the Christian religion in itself and as such, we certainly would have to say that without the fact of God speaking loudly on its behalf a religion other than Christianity could be the right and true one. But once the fact of God is there and its judgment has been enacted, we can no longer look at the Christian religion in itself and as such, and we can therefore put that levelling thought to use only afterwards as an expression of the fact that we confront the just acquittal that has happened to the Christian religion in this judgment wholly without pointing to any merit or worthiness on the basis of which we could confirm it. Rather, by accepting it and allowing it to be true, we can only cling wholly and utterly to the acquittal itself, or to the fact of God that proclaims it, and not at all to any kind of praiseworthy facts from the realm of the Christian religion itself. For just this reason, because the justification of the Christian religion is a *just* one, but one resting wholly and utterly in *God's* righteousness, and is not therefore in any way whatsoever an acquittal conditioned by any features of the Christian religion – for just this reason it can be understood by us in no other way than as an act of the *forgiveness of sin*. Because the Christian religion is justified by that fact of God, its various features, far from being adduced as the basis of its justification, are not even considered or taken into account but rather covered up. They must be covered up, they may not be considered or taken into account, after all, if there is to be an acquittal here. For the sum total of the features of even the Christian religion consists in the fact that it is idolatry and works-righteousness, faithlessness and therefore sin. It must be forgiven if it is to be justified. And we can only understand and accept its forgiveness if we understand and accept it as sheer forgiveness. For with any other interpretation and reception, we would once again peer beyond the fact of God, by which the Christian religion is justified, and by so doing we would once again forfeit the unconditioned nature of the knowledge of its truth. As forgiveness and only as forgiveness does the truth appropriate the Christian religion, and as forgiveness and only as forgiveness can the truth really be known as belonging inalienably to the Christian religion.

We ask: How then is this justification in the form of forgiveness an act of the righteousness and judgment of God? On the basis of what justice does God forgive – and forgive only here and not there? And we will certainly have to answer this question not only by referring to the freedom and inscrutability of divine judgment; we will at least have to bear in mind that this freedom and inscrutability is one with that of the revealed fact of God in the *name Jesus Christ*. It is already in order if there is forgiveness here and not there. It takes place, namely, according to the order of this fact of God, i.e., of the name Jesus Christ. It is what stands facing the world of the religions as the sun faces the earth. It denotes, however, a quite specific event, in which the world of the religions has a quite specific share. It denotes, namely, the becoming one of the eternal divine Word with human nature, and along with it the restoring of that nature – notwithstanding and in spite of its natural perversity – to humility and obedience to God. This restoration of human nature is the work of Jesus Christ from his birth to his death, which was revealed as such in his resurrection from the dead.

To the human nature restored in Jesus Christ, however, there also belongs the capacity of man from which, by virtue of his nature, only religion as faithlessness can and does in fact proceed. In Jesus Christ's human nature, man, instead of resisting God with idolatry and works-righteousness, has offered him the obedience of faith, and has therefore really satisfied the righteousness and judgment of God, really earned his acquittal and thus also the acquittal, the justification, of his religion. Now the Christian religion has to do with the earthly life of the church and the children of God, and therefore with the life of the earthly body of which Jesus Christ is the head, that is, with the life of those whom he has brought into fellowship with his human nature and thus into participation in the acquittal that he has rightly and justly earned. And the Christian religion is faith in following the justifying faith of Jesus Christ, which can be imitated by no one. If this is so, then the Christian religion, which as human faith surely needs forgiveness as much as the faith of any other religion, does in fact receive this forgiveness, and really does have it as well. And the forgiveness that it receives and enjoys is then in fact no arbitrary whim but rather a rigorous and just divine decision. Its object, to be sure, is first of all Jesus Christ alone, who as man has alone maintained and demonstrated that obedience of faith. But for the sake of Jesus Christ – i.e., for the sake of the fellowship and participation granted to men by Jesus Christ, for the sake of the solidarity of our humanity with his that he has given us, for the sake of his followers' faith in him – those whom he wills to call his brothers (along with their religion!) are now nevertheless also the object of that just divine decision, those who recognize and honour in him their firstborn brother in that faith as his followers. This acquittal will be for them – in contrast to him – free forgiveness unaccountably granted, forgiveness they have not earned, forgiveness for the sake of his merit, but forgiveness with all the gravity and import of a binding judicial decision, forgiveness that leaves nothing to be interpreted or overturned. And this unconditional forgiveness applies also to their religion, of which they would have to confess, were they able and willing to regard it in itself and as such, that it is faithlessness, like the faith of other religions.

The one decisive question above all that is posed to the Christian religion, that is, to its adherents and representatives, with regard to its truth is this: Who and what are they in their naked reality, as though standing before the all-perceiving eye of God? Really his church, his children, and therefore the adopted brothers of his eternal Son? If they are not, if their Christian religion is only a mask, then even if it be Christian religion in its most perfect and consistent form it is faithlessness like all the other paganisms, it is falsehood and wrong, an abomination before God. If they are – if they therefore live by God's grace, if they partake in the human nature of his eternal Son, if they are nourished by his body and blood as earthly members of his earthly body in fellowship with him as their heavenly Head

– then for the sake of this fellowship their sins are forgiven, then the sin of their religion is also rightly forgiven. Then their Christian religion is the justified religion, and therefore the right religion, and therefore the true religion. The fact of God in the name Jesus Christ then confirms, beyond all dialectic and excluding any discussion, what no other fact does or can confirm: the creation and election of their particular religion as the one, the only, true religion. The Christian religion and its adherents and representatives cannot, to be sure, be spared that one decisive question. Nor can it ever become irrelevant to the present; it can never be left behind as already settled. Whenever Christianity confronts the other religions, whenever a Christian confronts the believer of another religion, this question stands over him like a sword. From this perspective one can and must say that the Christian religion, standing in the midst of the world of the religions, is more endangered, more defenceless, and weaker than any other religion. It either has its justification in the name Jesus Christ or it doesn't have it at all. And this justification must occur in the reality of life, of the church and the children of God. The occurrence of this life, however, is grace, the grace of the Word, which begets the faith of his disciples, and begets for himself his church and his children, according to his free, unaccountable mercy. The possibility of a negative answer to that question is the abyss at the edge of which the truth of the Christian religion is decided. But in answering that question positively, the latter question is also answered positively: the Christian religion is plucked out of the world of the religions, and out of the judgment and sentence pronounced upon it, like a brand from the burning.[20] There men are not vindicated against other men, nor one part of humanity against other parts of the same humanity, but rather God against and for all men, the whole of humanity. That they accept and approve this fact is the advantage and the glory of Christianity, the light and the honour in which their particular religion comes to stand. And just as it has not taken this light and glory for itself, so also no one can take it away, and so it and only it has the task and authority for *mission*, that is, to confront the world of all religions as the one true religion, to invite and to call upon them with complete self-confidence to turn back from their ways, to turn to the Christian way.

The Christian religion will always be viable, healthy, and strong to the degree that it possesses this *self-confidence*. It will always possess this self-confidence, however, only to the degree that its believers and proclaimers are able to look away from themselves to the *fact of God*, which alone justifies. To the degree to which at the same time they want to rely on other facts as well, this self-confidence will secretly suffer one crack after another and must finally fail altogether. And it makes no difference whether these other facts consist in ecclesiastical institutions, in theological systems, in inner experiences, in moral transformations in the lives of individual believers, or in world-altering effects of Christianity as a whole. The sidelong glance at such facts will always in the long run result

120

in uncertainty, and indeed very quickly, regarding the truth of the Christian religion. For all these things may indeed be facts, but without exception they are facts that are first in need of justification themselves and thus cannot be used as the basis for it. If the Christian or the Christians, in enquiring after the truth of their religion, are first concerned with themselves and with Christianity, without remembering that in this sphere they can only have to do with forgiven sin, then let them just see how long they will be able to defend themselves against the overpowering scepticism regarding the truth question that will rise up within themselves. And if they can do it, if they are in a position to impute to those facts a credibility that they cannot possibly have in this sphere, that will be far worse for them and for the Christian religion than any open outbreak and admission of doubt. Once more: those who believe in their church and those who believe in their theology, those who believe in the transformed human being and those who believe in improved relationships, are here all on the same path, the path to uncertainty. And this is betrayed by the fact that all of them must seek refuge – casually but openly, and with the incorrigible tenacity of those who secretly despair of faith – in reason or in culture or in humanity or in ethnicity, in order to provide some support or other to the Christian religion. It will not be possible to support the Christian religion from without, however, if it can no longer stand on its own. If it were standing on its own, it would refuse to be supported from without. Standing on its own, it would indeed be standing on the fact of God that justifies it, and on it alone. All other attempts at support would then be left out of consideration as a waste of time and energy – indeed, as a resumption of that faithlessness which God does not regard or take into account but rather covers up and forgives. They cannot be left out of consideration, however, once the sidelong glance at other facts besides the fact of God, which alone justifies, has occurred. Faithlessness is then once again on the agenda, once again has the decisive word, and it will see in such attempts at support not a waste of time and energy but serious, urgent necessities. The secularization of Christianity will then be fully under way, and no subjective piety will be capable of halting its onward march. And precisely its viability, health, and strength with regard to the *outer* world will then be at an end.

4. The relationship between the name Jesus Christ and the Christian religion has to do with an act of divine *sanctification*. We said that in seeking the basis for asserting the truth of the Christian religion we could, to begin with, only look past the religion itself to the act of God on which it is based, and that we would have to come back again and again to this 'to begin with'. Now when we enquire into this truth, we can certainly never look anywhere except at this act of God, not even just in passing. We cannot try to seek the justification of the Christian religion apart from the name Jesus Christ in some other facts, nor in any inner or outer justified state of the Christian religion in itself and as such. But this very justification of the Christian religion through the name Jesus Christ alone obviously signifies a certain positive relationship between the two, a relationship in which the Christian religion is differentiated and singled out from other religions by the name Jesus Christ, formed and shaped by it, and claimed for its service,

becoming the historical manifestation and means of its revelation. We have compared the name Jesus Christ with the sun facing the earth. That must be the end of the matter. But the sun shines, and its light does not remain something remote and alien to the earth; rather, without ceasing to be the sun's light, it becomes the earth's, the light illumining the earth, which, in itself lightless, now becomes, not a second sun, but yet the bearer of the reflected sunlight and thus an enlightened earth. In the same way, the name Jesus Christ, because it alone is the justification of the Christian religion, cannot transcend it without also becoming immanent within it. Because the Christian religion and it alone is justified by that name, it is differentiated and singled out, stamped and characterized by that name in a specific way unique to itself. In the light of its justification, its creation and election by the name Jesus Christ, the fact that it is this particular religion, the Christian religion and no other, cannot possibly be just a neutral, trivial, meaningless, or dumb fact. Rather, the Christian religion, although in itself it is a religion like all others, is meaningful and articulate, a sign and a declaration. Corresponding to the event on God's side – though it is the side of the incarnate Word of God, the God who has accepted man and given himself to man – is a quite specific event on man's side, though one wholly determined by the Word of God, an existence and a form in the midst of the world of human religion, standing out as such from everything having existence and form in this sphere. This correspondence is the relationship between the name Jesus Christ and the Christian religion from the standpoint of its sanctification. It is not by the laws and powers inherent in human religion and therefore in man but rather by virtue of divine endowment and appointment that this particular existence and this particular form will become an event in the midst of the world of human religion. What there becomes an event, unjustified as it is in itself, will have no independent role or significance but will have only to serve the name Jesus Christ, which alone justifies it. It will never be able to replace and displace this name with its own substance – not even in passing – but it will only be able to witness to it, it will only be able to awaken and keep alive the remembrance and expectation of it. It will never be able to claim to be itself the act of God indicated by this name; it will always be willing and able only to be its warning and comforting sign. It will take part in the truth only to the precise extent that it points to and proclaims it. And even in this pointing and proclaiming it will neither have nor claim any power and authority of its own; rather, it will speak but also keep silence, work but also rest, be known but also not known by virtue of the power and authority of the name Jesus Christ effected in the outpouring of the Holy Spirit. That name and it alone will be the power and the mystery of the declaration that is the meaning of this particular existence and form. It and it alone will bring to utterance this existence and form as the existence and form of the true religion. It is not justified because it is holy in itself

– it is not – but because it is justified, it is therefore also sanctified, made holy. And so also it is not true because it is holy in itself – it is not, nor will it ever be – but rather it is sanctified, made holy, in order now to show that it is the true religion. Here we come upon what we earlier described as the twofold subjective reality of revelation, which corresponds in our realm to the objective revelation in Jesus Christ. It is the Christian religion: the *sacramental* space created by the Holy Spirit in which God, whose Word has become flesh, continues to speak through the signs of his revelation; and the *existence of human beings*, created by the same Holy Spirit, who continue to hear this God speaking in his revelation. The existence of the church and the children of God in their particular, quite unassuming reality, which is nevertheless visible to everyone and meaningful in its visibility, and which is called and equipped to declare the name Jesus Christ – that is the sanctification of the Christian religion.

The covenant of God founded on grace and election acquired right away, already with his people Israel, this witness of a visible form, a seal perceivable by the obedient as well as the disobedient, by Israel itself as well as the gentiles, through the establishment of the *law*. The law was supposed and intended to be nothing other than a sign of Yahweh's grace and election. But precisely as a sign of Yahweh's grace and election, as a witness to the covenant, the law was supposed and intended to be observed, kept, studied day and night. The founding of the covenant did not take place through the establishment of the law, let alone through the fact that the law was honoured, studied, and observed by Israel, but rather prior to the law through the repeatedly confirmed calling of Abraham, Isaac, and Jacob, through the sending of Moses, through the liberation of Israel from Egypt. Because it took place, however, as the founding of the covenant of God with this people, which like all other peoples existed in human history, it did not take place without the establishment of the law, without claiming this people for obedience to the law, without the promise of curse or blessing attached to its observance or non-observance. That precisely this people was the people of the covenant needed to be verified again and again in the validity and observance of the law. It was the gift of the law, the sanctification of this people – corresponding to the grace of Yahweh and necessarily following immediately from the revelation of grace as its necessary historical form that could not be separated from it – its selection, differentiation, and distinction as *this* people. How was it able to exist both as a human and historical people and yet simultaneously as the people of Yahweh, unless this visible selection, differentiation, and distinction had simultaneously befallen it? And how was it able to experience and accept the grace that had befallen it with its existence as *this* people, without being continually mindful of this visible selection, differentiation, and distinction and without continually acknowledging it? Clearly all observance of the law could also have been only a sign and witness, relative only to the gratitude for the assurance, 'I am the Lord your God!' which could never be exhausted even by the strictest observance of any one of its commandments. But in this relation it was obviously a necessary sign and witness, whose omission immediately called that gratitude into question, and with it their existence as *this* people, automatically transforming that assurance into a threat.

Now to this there corresponds something else. According to the New Testament, there is not only the reconciliation of the world with God in Jesus Christ but also along with this reconciliation itself, and as its immediately necessary annexe, a 'ministry of reconciliation': the establishment of a 'word of reconciliation', a human plea included in and with the reconciliation accomplished by God in Jesus Christ: 'Be reconciled to God!' (2 Cor. 5:18f.). It is a ministry 'as we have received mercy' (2 Cor. 4:1), a 'ministry of the Spirit' (2 Cor. 3:8), a 'ministry of righteousness' (2 Cor. 3:9). It consists in this, and only in this, that men may 'with unveiled face *reflect*' the glory of the Lord (2 Cor. 3:18; cf. 1 Cor. 13:12). The point is clear: 'What we proclaim is not ourselves, but Jesus Christ as Lord' (2 Cor. 4:5). It is therefore a strictly subordinate, relative event, utterly bound by the divine act of justification, and by the divine creation and election that are its foundation, and utterly dependent on it. Where would the image in the mirror be, even for just an instant, without the object facing the mirror? Where would the reflected light of the earth illumined by the sun be without the sun itself? Even though bound and dependent in this way, however, it is a real and necessary event, which takes place in this 'ministry of reconciliation', and without 'losing heart' (2 Cor. 4:1; 4:16), this ministry must therefore be accomplished with 'joyfulness' (2 Cor. 3:12).[21] It is the sanctification of the community formed by God's revelation and reconciliation, replacing the Old Testament law, that takes place in this event. It is the sanctification of the Christian religion, accomplished once and for all in the name Jesus Christ and again and again to be acknowledged and affirmed in obedience: we really do have the whole problem immediately before our eyes in the sanctification of the New Testament apostolic office as described by Paul. From this perspective we can see the need to take seriously the fact that this religion has a concrete historical existence and form: distinguishing its existence and form from those of other religions, the problems of its existence and form, the possibility and the danger of going astray with regard to them, and the task of repeatedly making decisions regarding them. In view of the fact that the name Jesus Christ is not only the justification but also the sanctification of the Christian religion, all of this has to be taken just as seriously as Israel had to take its law if it wanted to be and remain the people of the covenant; it has therefore to be taken seriously in faith and obedience to the justifying name Jesus Christ, and thereby in the inescapable light of the question of truth, which is posed and must be answered again and again. The name Jesus Christ, which justifies the Christian religion without its being able as a human religion to contribute even in the slightest to this reconciliation – this name is at the same time the authority and power that moves it in its wholly human sinfulness and transforms it, which continually erects and maintains signs in its domain and claims recognition. It is the authority and power which through these signs – through the sign of the church, and through the sign of the existence of the children of God gathered together as the church – continually acts as a comfort and a warning to this religion in its history, whose revelation not only was, but through the ministry of these signs is also revelation today, and will be revelation tomorrow. That Christians are sinners, and the church a church of sinners, is quite clear. But justified sinners

– and that's what Christians are – are also thereby, by virtue of the same Word and Spirit that justifies them, sanctified – that is, sinners brought under discipline, placed under the order of revelation; sinners who are no longer free in all their sinfulness but remember the Lord who justifies them and for whom they must wait; sinners who, to this extent, although they are sinners, are ready for him and stand at his disposal. This is just what Christian religion as a historical form means, in general and in particular: readiness for the Lord, by whose name those who profess this religion, and along with them their religion as such, are created, elected, and justified. And in just this way the problems of the existence and form of this religion become serious problems: the question of canon and dogma, the question of confessions and creeds, of worship and church polity, the question of correct theology, of correct piety, and correct Christian ethics. They do not become serious problems because the Christian religion might be able to justify itself as the true religion by managing to answer or solve them in this or that particular way, which it may bring itself to do now and again, but rather because in answering these problems it is again and again decided whether the Christian religion is still ready here and now for the Lord who long ago justified it, whether it is in fact the already justified and therefore true religion, whether it still participates, and participates anew, in the promise made long ago and valid apart from its merit or cooperation. It is not a matter of acquiring and maintaining an advantage when Christians, and Christianity, enquire after the truth concerning the visible existence and form of their religion, and when they suffer and struggle over the truth already known. The fact remains that they can gain no advantage even with the best possible results of such working, suffering, and struggling. It all amounts to this, that just as they have to breathe again and again for the sake of their animal life, so also they must always put into practice anew their existence as Christians and Christianity, they must be the ones who already have the advantage of knowing the name Jesus Christ and being the ones named after him. It is a matter of the practice and repetition of their existence as church and children of God. They would not be what they are from eternity and in eternity, unless they were so also in time; they would not be what they are invisibly unless they were so visibly, and therefore in this practice and repetition. Their sanctification, however, which they undergo in this practice and repetition, is beyond their own effort and its success or failure; it is, no less than their justification, the work of him for whose sake they are called Christians and Christianity.

Notes

TRANSLATOR'S PREFACE

1. Georg Wilhelm Friedrich Hegel, *Lectures on the Philosophy of Religion*, 3 vols., ed. Peter C. Hodgson, trans. R. F. Brown *et al.* (Berkeley and Los Angeles: University of California Press, 1984–85), 1:57.
2. Readers wishing to pursue the theological implications of these gender-related issues may wish to look at my article 'The Gender of God and the Theology of Metaphor', in *Speaking the Christian God: The Holy Trinity and the Challenge of Feminism*, ed. Alvin F. Kimel, Jr. (Grand Rapids, MI: Wm. B. Eerdmans Publishing Co., 1992), 44–64.
3. <http://forum.leo.org/cgi-bin/dict/forum.cgi>

INTRODUCTION

1. Hans W. Frei, 'An Afterword: Eberhard Busch's Biography of Karl Barth', in *Karl Barth in Re-View: Posthumous Works Reviewed and Assessed*, ed. H.-Martin Rumscheidt (Pittsburgh, PA: Pickwick Press, 1981), 97.
2. For a full account of Barth's life, see Eberhard Busch, *Karl Barth: His Life from Letters and Autobiographical Texts*, trans. John Bowden, 2nd ed. rev. (Philadelphia: Fortress Press, 1976). Shorter overviews of his life and work appear in Joseph L. Mangina, *Karl Barth: Theologian of Christian Witness* (Louisville, KY: Westminster John Knox Press, 2004), ch. 1; and John Webster, *Barth* (London; New York: Continuum, 2000), ch. 1.
3. Barth, 'Evangelical Theology in the 19th Century', in *The Humanity of God* (Richmond, VA: John Knox Press, 1960), 14.
4. Karl Barth, *Der Römerbrief (Erste Fassung), 1919*, ed. Hermann Schmidt, vol. 2 of *Karl Barth Gesamtausgabe: Akademische Werke* (Zurich: Theologischer Verlag Zürich, 1985).
5. Mangina (*Karl Barth*, 3) cites this phrase from Karl Adam, writing in the Roman Catholic monthly *Das Hochland*, June 1926, 276–7.

6. Barth, *Anselm, Fides Quaerens Intellectum: Anselm's Proof of the Existence of God in the Context of His Theological Scheme* (London: SCM Press, 1960), 16.

7. Barth, *Evangelical Theology: An Introduction* (New York: Holt, Rinehart & Winston, 1963), 49.

8. Cited from a letter by Barth in Busch, *Karl Barth*, 255.

9. Busch, *Karl Barth*, 498.

10. Robert W. Jenson, 'Karl Barth', in *The Modern Theologians*, 2nd ed., edited by David F. Ford (Cambridge, MA, and Oxford: Blackwell, 1997), 22.

11. J. Glenn Gray, Introduction to G. W. F. Hegel, *On Art, Religion, Philosophy* (New York: Harper & Row, 1970), 14–15. I have just one quibble with this account of *Aufhebung*: its outcome is not so much a *blend* as a *reconfiguration* of old and new; the change is not merely quantitative but qualitative. For this reason I would also eschew the term 'synthesis', which Hegel rarely if ever employs in this context.

12. In Karl Barth, *The Word of God and the Word of Man*, trans. Douglas Horton (New York: Harper & Row, 1957), 28–50. Subsequent page references to this volume will be given parenthetically in the text.

13. The most prominent example is Harnack's Berlin lectures of 1900 on 'The Essence of Christianity', translated by Thomas Bailey Saunders as *What Is Christianity?* (New York: Harper & Row, 1957).

14. Barth, 'Vorwort zum Nachdruck dieses Buches [1963]', in *Römerbrief (Erste Fassung)*, 6.

15. Barth, *The Epistle to the Romans*, trans. Edwyn C. Hoskyns (New York: Oxford University Press, 1968), 253 (translating *Römerbrief [1922]*, 257). This translation, originally published in 1933, is based on the 6th German ed. (virtually unchanged from the 1922 ed.), was largely responsible for making Barth known in the English-speaking world. Subsequent page references to this work will be given parenthetically.

16. *Römerbrief (1922)*, 233; cf. *Romans*, 231. Though Hoskyns successfully renders Barth's exuberant style, he often paraphrases his German rather than translating it directly. For this reason I have employed my own more literal translation of this and subsequent passages (but in each case I have also indicated the corresponding passage in the Hoskins translation).

17. *Römerbrief (1922)*, 256; cf. *Romans*, 253.

18. *Römerbrief (1922)*, 257–8; cf. *Romans*, 254.

19. *Römerbrief (1922)*, 273 (Barth's emphasis); cf. *Romans*, 268.

20. Barth, *Die christliche Dogmatik im Entwurf*, vol. 1: *Die Lehre vom Worte Gottes: Prolegomena zur christlichen Dogmatik* (Munich: Chr. Kaiser Verlag, 1927).

21. Barth, *How I Changed My Mind*, 42–3.
22. Barth, *Fides Quaerens Intellectum: Anselms Beweis der Existenz Gottes im Zusammenhang seines theologischen Programms* (Munich: C. Kaiser, 1931); English trans.: *Anselm, Fides Quaerens Intellectum: Anselm's Proof of the Existence of God in the Context of His Theological Scheme* (London: SCM Press, 1960).
23. The key texts in their debate, Brunner's *Natur und Gnade* and Barth's *Nein!*, are included in Walther Fürst, ed., *'Dialektische Theologie' in Scheidung und Bewährung 1933–1936* (Munich: Chr. Kaiser Verlag, 1966), 169–258. A translation by Peter Fraenkel of both the Brunner and Barth texts, originally published as *Natural Theology* (London: Geoffrey Bles, 1946), has recently been reissued by Wipf and Stock (2002).
24. Barth, *How I Changed My Mind*, 43.
25. Barth, 'The Humanity of God', in *The Humanity of God*, 38–65, esp. 38–46.
26. Barth, 'Humanity of God', 45.
27. Barth, 'Humanity of God', 46.
28. Barth, 'Humanity of God', 48.
29. The prototype of such theological prolegomena is the extended introduction to Friedrich Schleiermacher's classic work of modern Protestant dogmatics, *The Christian Faith*, ed. H. R. Mackintosh and J. S. Stewart, 2 vols. (New York: Harper & Row, 1963).
30. Barth, 'Gottes Offenbarung als Aufhebung der Religion', in *Die kirchliche Dogmatik* (Zurich: Theologischer Verlag, 1932–67), § 17 (vol. 1/2, pp. 304–97). For the published English translation, see *Church Dogmatics*, vol. 1/2, ed. G. W. Bromiley and T. F. Torrance, trans. G. T. Thomson and Harold Knight (Edinburgh: T&T Clark, 1956), pp. 280–361. Page references to the new translation of this text in the present volume will be made parenthetically.
31. This statement suggests that the title of part three, 'Die wahre Religion', is best translated with the definite article, even though German usage permits either alternative in English. In view of Barth's penchant for emphasizing dialectical opposites, I think his meaning is best brought out by the jarring juxtaposition of 'Religion as Faithlessness' and '*The* True Religion'. Needless to say, he would not have been impressed by the objection that the latter has an 'exclusivist' ring to it.
32. I have heard such views attributed to Barth more often than one might suppose, and not only by secular scholars of religion but also by Christian theologians.
33. For a discussion of the 'postmodern turn' in religious studies, see [p. 25] above.

34. This methodological principle in Barth's theology appears less idiosyncratic today, since the rise of philosophical antifoundationalism. See my discussion of this issue in *Imagining God: Theology and the Religious Imagination* (Grand Rapids, MI: Eerdmans, 1998), 36–40.

35. Barth describes the characteristic mode of thought of scripture as 'the *circulus virtuosus* [*jener heilsame Zirkel*] in which it always moves in the matter of truth' (*KD* 4/3: 102; *CD* 4/3: 92). See also *KD* 1/1: 954–90 (*CD* 1/1: 853–84), and *KD* 3/1: 401–15 (*CD* 3/1: 350–63), where he calls Descartes' proof for the existence of God a *circulus vitiosus* and contrasts it with the proper circularity of a proof like Anselm's that is based on God's self-revelation.

36. Freud defines religious ideas as 'illusions, fulfilments of the oldest, strongest and most urgent wishes of mankind'. *The Future of an Illusion* trans. and ed. James Strachey (New York: W. W. Norton & Co., 1961), 38.

37. The translation in the *Church Dogmatics* – 'singular, perhaps, but not unique' – is misleading since 'singular', like 'unique', means one of a kind. It also misses Barth's confident tone: he says not 'perhaps' but 'to be sure' (*zwar ... aber doch nicht*).

38. Ingolf U. Dalferth, in an otherwise superb essay, mistakes Barth's insistence on the unavoidability of religion. After claiming quite accurately that for Barth 'theology can in no way be built on the fact of religion', he continues: 'There may be religion without corresponding faith; and there may be Christian faith without there being religion.' The first statement is obviously true, but the second misses Barth's insistence on the religious form of divine revelation. Dalferth's claim that Barth, like Dietrich Bonhoeffer, believed that the 'Christian faith is not bound to exist in the form of religion' is therefore questionable. Dalferth, 'Karl Barth's Eschatological Realism', in *Karl Barth: Centenary Essays*, ed. S. W. Sykes (New York: Cambridge University Press, 1989), 40.

39. Barth elaborates the historical thesis to which he here alludes in 'Man in the Eighteenth Century', the opening chapter of *Protestant Thought: From Rousseau to Ritschl* (1971; reprint Salem, NH: Ayer Co., 1987), 11–57.

40. This claim is a strong one, to be sure, but not in the sense implied by the translation in the *Church Dogmatics* ('revelation is denied when it is regarded as open to discussion'), which appears to preclude all discussion about the meaning of revelation. Barth rules out only the treatment of revelation as *problematic* (i.e., possibly invalid), since theology is based on divine revelation and thus cannot call it into question without self-contradiction.

41. The rendering of *Geschichte* by 'history' in the *Church Dogmatics* ('The only thing we can do is to recount the history of the relationships between the two') rather than 'story' or 'narrative'

leaves the false impression that historians, or perhaps biblical scholars using historical-critical method, might fulfil the theological task. For Barth's distinction between *Geschichte* and *Historie*, see my article 'Myth, History, and Imagination: The Creation Narratives in Bible and Theology', *Horizons in Biblical Theology* 12 (December 1990): 19–38, 61–3.

42. Here, as in other citations, the emphasis is Barth's own. In the *Church Dogmatics*, the use of 'abolition' in this key sentence undercuts Barth's analogical point by emphasizing only one side (the negative) of the dialectic. The term *Aufhebung* recurs at the key points of transition in Barth's argument, here and at the end of part two. By using different English terms for the various occurrences of *Aufhebung* and its cognates, the original translators obscure the central role of the title concept and distort the meaning of individual passages.

43. By translating *Wesen* as 'nature', the *Church Dogmatics* obscures Barth's allusion to the nineteenth-century quest for the 'essence' of religion. The most notorious example of the genre is Ludwig Feuerbach's book *The Essence of Christianity*, and Barth surely has in mind also Adolf von Harnack's epitome of liberal theology, his lectures in 1900 on 'The Essence of Christianity' (trans. *What Is Christianity?*; see note above).

44. By translating *'heidnisch'* with the archaic term 'heathen' and omitting Barth's scare quotes around it, the original translators of the *Church Dogmatics* added one more brush stroke to the caricature of Barth as the arrogant Christian imperialist. They also refer mistakenly to 'Reformed Christianity'; Barth's term (*reformatorisch*) includes all the major branches of the Protestant Reformation.

45. Emile Durkheim, *The Elementary Forms of the Religious Life*, trans. Joseph Ward Swain (New York: Free Press, 1965), 477.

46. Sigmund Freud, *The Future of an Illusion*, trans. James Strachey (New York: W. W. Norton & Co., 1961), 71.

47. Barth addresses the scientific nature of theology in the opening pages of the *Church Dogmatics*. For a critical appraisal of his position, see Wolfhart Pannenberg, *Theology and the Philosophy of Science*, trans. Francis McDonagh (Philadelphia: Westminster Press, 1976), 265–76. The issues raised are complex and go beyond the scope of the present discussion.

48. William James, *The Varieties of Religious Experience* (New York: Longmans, Green & Co., 1923), 31; original in italics.

49. Durkheim, 62; original in italics.

50. Wilfred Cantwell Smith, *Religious Diversity*, ed. Willard G. Oxtoby (New York: Harper & Row, 1976), 22–40. Smith is less convincing when he goes on to theorize rather vaguely about a 'faith' that transcends the particular truth criteria of concrete religious traditions.

51. The phrase 'hermeneutics of suspicion' was coined by Paul Ricoeur, who identifies Marx, Nietzsche, and Freud as the 'masters of suspicion'. See *Freud and Philosophy: An Essay on Interpretation*, trans. Denis Savage (New Haven, CT: Yale University Press, 1970), 32–6.

52. David Bentley Hart captures the gist of what he calls the 'great project of "modernity"' in a felicitous and pithy definition: 'the search for comprehensive metanarratives and epistemological foundations by way of a neutral and unaided rationality, available to all reflective intellects, and independent of cultural and linguistic conditions'. *The Beauty of the Infinite: The Aesthetics of Christian Truth* (Grand Rapids, MI: Eerdmans, 2003), 3.

53. William E. Paden's textbook *Interpreting the Sacred: Ways of Viewing Religion* (Boston: Beacon, 1992), offers an accessible and lucid account of religious studies after the postmodern turn. 'The capacity to see one's view of the world *as* a view', he writes, 'is a mark of contemporary thinking' (3). Paden's book is a welcome contribution by a scholar trained in the history of religions – a classic 'outsider' approach – who not only demonstrates the 'theory-laden' nature of 'scientific' theories of religion but also takes seriously the 'insider' tradition – what he calls 'religious interpretations of religion' (see esp. ch. 6).

54. Two of the newest textbooks in religious studies show that the canon continues to operate in the same old way: Ivan Strenski, *Thinking about Religion: An Historical Introduction to Theories of Religion* (New York: Blackwell, 2006) and the second edition of Daniel L. Pals, *Eight Theories of Religion* (New York: Oxford University Press, 2006). Both books present the views of the usual 'outsider' theorists, mostly from the social sciences (the newcomer to this edition of the Pals book is Max Weber).

55. A notable exception is J. Samuel Preus, *Explaining Religion: Criticism and Theory from Bodin to Freud* (New Haven, CT: Yale University Press, 1987). In tracing the 'paradigm shift' that brought about the 'birth of the modern study of religion', Preus identifies the question of *origins* as the 'key issue'. Whereas the hallmark of the 'theological' approach is its claim that religion can explain itself, the 'alternative tradition' stemming from the Enlightenment accounts for religion in exclusively naturalistic terms. The question of origins, in fact, 'divides theology from the study of religion' (69). Preus thus excludes theologians from religious studies by fiat: 'The study of religion issues from *criticism* of religion' (82). But this sharp division is possible only because Preus assumes throughout that only theological interpreters of religion are motivated by 'personal commitments, apologetic interests, and political convenience' (xviii), without acknowledging analogous motivations in those who 'turn from a theological to a scientific paradigm for the study of

religion' (84). Preus's explicit appeal to concepts like 'paradigm' and 'research tradition' from recent philosophy of science ought to have alerted him to the unacknowledged commitments of those who follow a scientific paradigm. To acknowledge this situation, however, would undermine his claim that only religious 'outsiders' are qualified to explain religion truthfully.

56. Russell T. McCutcheon, *Critics Not Caretakers: Redescribing the Public Study of Religion* (Albany: State University of New York Press, 2001), 103–4. See the perceptive response to McCutcheon by Tyler Roberts in 'Exposure and Explanation: On the New Protectionism in the Study of Religion' (*Journal of the American Academy of Religion* 72 [2004]): 143–72.

1. THE PROBLEM OF RELIGION IN THEOLOGY

1. Cf., for what follows, Edvard Lehmann, 'Die Erscheinungs- und Ideenwelt der Religion' [The phenomenal and ideal world of religion], in Chantepie de la Saussaye, *Lehrbuch der Religionsgeschichte*, 1925, vol. I, pp. 23–130. [An English translation of this work was published as P. D. Chantepie de la Saussaye, *Manual of the Science of Religion* (New York: Longmans, Green, New York, 1891) (trans.).]

2. *Die christliche Glaubenslehre* [The Christian doctrine of faith], vol. I, 1840, p. 352.

3. *Calvin: Institutes of the Christian Religion* 1. 2. 2; trans. Ford Lewis Battles, 2 vols., Library of Christian Classics (Philadelphia: Westminster, 1960), 1:43.

4. *Comp. Theol. Pos.* [Compendium of revealed theology], 1686, Prol I 7 f.

5. A. Polanus, *Synt. Theol.* [Definition of Christian theology], 1609, pp. 3694f.

6. This passage could also be translated: 'The true religion alone is properly so called; other religions are called religion, but they are not'. Polanus plays upon two meanings of the Latin term *religio*, which can refer to religion as devotion or to religion as one cult among many. *Trans.*

7. *Christ. Theol. Comp.* [Compendium of Christian theology], 1626, II 4, 1.

8. Ibid., 4, 3.

9. *Loci comm.* [Commonplaces of sacred theology], 1640, p. 31f.

10. *Synopsis purioris Theol.* [Leiden Synopsis], Leiden, 1624 (*Disp.* 2, 17–20; this disputation took place under the chairmanship of this same Walaeus!)

11. *Syn.* [Leiden Synopsis] 2, 18.
12. Walaeus p. 32.
13. *Institutes* 1. 6-8; LCC 1:69-92.
14. *Institutes* 1. 8. 13; LCC 1:92.
15. *Corp. Theol. chr.* [Corpus of Christian theology], 1676, L I S. 7f.
16. *Chr. Theol. lib. duo* [Great system of Christian theology in two books], 1634, 1: 1.
17. E.g., in A. Calov, *Syst. loc. theol.* [System of theological topics] I, 1655, c 2.; in J. F. König, *theologiae pos. accroam.* [Secrets of revealed theology], 1664, § 57 f.; in A. Quenstedt, *Theol. did. pol.* [Didactic-polemical theology], 1685, I 2.
18. *C. 2 sut. 2 q. 6.*
19. *Ex. theol. acroam.* [Secrets of revealed theology], 1707.
20. Christoph Matthäus Pfaff, *Einl. in d. Dogmat. Theol.* [Introduction to dogmatic theology], 1747, pp. 27f., cited by A. F. Stolzenburg, *Die Theol. des Jo. Franc. Buddeus und des Chr. Matth. Pfaff* [The theology of Johann Franz Buddeus and Christoph Matthäus Pfaff], 1926, pp. 219f.
21. The 'German Christians' (Deutsche Christen) were the pro-Nazi party within the German Evangelical Church, against whose teachings the *Theological Declaration of Barmen* (of which Barth was the primary author) was directed in 1934. *Trans.*
22. Barth's term here (a favourite of his) is not *Objektivität*, the kind of objectivity that stands in contrast to subjectivity, but rather *Sachlichkeit*, the objectivity of the thinker who never loses sight of *die Sache*, the actual subject matter at hand. *Trans.*
23. Barth's word is '*religionswissenschaftlich*' (in quotes); he is referring to theologians who are oriented towards religious studies or the 'scientific study of religion'. *Trans.*

2. RELIGION AS FAITHLESSNESS

1. G. E. Lessing's drama *Nathan the Wise* (1779), which contains the famous parable of the three rings, is one of the most influential expressions of the Enlightenment view of religious toleration. For a discussion of its content and implications, see James C. Livingston, *Modern Christian Thought*, 2nd ed. (Upper Saddle River, NJ: Prentice Hall, 1997), 1:11. *Trans.*
2. *Lessing's Theological Writings*, trans. Henry Chadwick (Stanford, CA: Stanford University Press, 1957), 98. *Trans.*
3. Barth's term *Unglaube*, the key to this part of his argument, is typically translated 'unbelief' (as in the English version of the *Church Dogmatics*). The German word *Glaube*, however, does service for what in English is called both *belief* and *faith*. The context of Barth's

use of the term shows that he is charging religion not primarily with the holding of false beliefs but rather with a lack of faith – of what Luther (one of Barth's sources here) calls *fiducia*, believing God's promises. For this reason I have consistently rendered *Unglaube* as 'faithlessness'.

4. *Luther's Works*, vol. 30: *The Catholic Epistles*, ed. Jaroslav Pelikan (St Louis: Concordia Publishing House, 1967), pp. 36–7. *Trans.*

5. Barth's verb *aufgehoben* might well be translated 'suspended' in the immediate context of this sentence. But he surely intends also to recall the *Aufhebung* – sublimation – of the main title of § 17. The dialectical relationship of 'could'–'cannot'–'can' does, after all, recapitulate precisely the central logic of the whole essay, a logic which he tries to capture in the quasi-Hegelian concept of *Aufhebung*. *Trans.*

6. *Institutes* 1. 11. 8; LCC 1:108; trans. rev. *Trans.*

7. *Institutes* 1. 11. 1; LCC 1:100. *Trans.*

8. *Institutes* 1. 11. 1; LCC 1:100; trans. rev. *Trans.*

9. *Institutes* 1. 4. 1; LCC 1:47. *Trans.*

10. John Calvin, *Commentary on the Gospel According to John*, trans. William Pringle (Edinburgh: Calvin Translation Society, 1847); reprinted in *Calvin's Commentaries*, vol. 17 (Grand Rapids, MI: Baker Book House, 1993), p. 113. *Trans.*

11. This sentence relates two of Barth's most important and controversial ideas. By denying that revelation 'hooks up with' religion (*knüpft ... an*), he is restating his argument about the so-called point of contact (*Anknüpfungspunkt*) for revelation from his famous debate with Emil Brunner. For a discussion of their dispute, see Garrett Green, *Imagining God* (Grand Rapids, MI: Eerdmans, 1998), 29–33. The other issue is once again the title concept of sublimation (*Aufhebung*). In this context, the negative aspect of sublimation (suspension, or even abolition) comes to the fore, but for Barth the relationship is always a dialectical one. It is noteworthy here that Barth not only repeats his central thesis that revelation sublimates religion but also states explicitly that religion sublimates revelation. *Trans.*

12. Barth refers to the literal meaning of Paul's term *deisidaimonia*, which can mean 'superstition' but in this passage is usually rendered 'religiousness'. *Trans.*

13. W. A. 30 II 186, 15.

14. *Cruc. Comm. Post.*, 1545, W. A. 21, 365, 12.

15. Cf. Theodosius Harnack, *Luthers Theologie*, 1862; new ed. 1927, vol. 1, pp. 450ff.

16. Martin Luther, 'Preface to the Epistle of St. Paul to the Romans', in *Luther's Works*, vol. 35, ed. E. Theodore Bachmann (Philadelphia: Muhlenberg Press, 1960), p. 380. *Trans.*

17. This technical term means 'advisory' or 'hortatory'; Barth is referring to those passages where Paul exhorts his readers or gives them advice. *Trans.*

18. Barth is alluding to a famous passage in the conclusion to Kant's *Critique of Practical Reason*: 'Two things fill the mind with ever new and increasing admiration and awe, the oftener and more steadily we reflect on them: the starry heavens above me and the moral law within me' (trans. Lewis White Beck [Indianapolis and New York: Bobbs-Merrill, 1956], 166). *Trans.*

19. By saying that the need is 'kein schlechthinniges', Barth may be alluding to Schleiermacher's famous definition of religion as 'schlechthinniges Abhängigkeitsgefühl', the feeling of absolute (or utter) dependence. *Trans.*

20. See n. 18 above. *Trans.*

21. Barth's use of the phrase *Blut und Boden*, an unmistakable reference to the Nazi slogan, is a reminder how much his negative characterization of religion owes to his recent experience of the attempt by the 'German Christians' to co-opt the Christian churches for religio-political purposes of the National Socialist movement. *Trans.*

22. Probably an allusion to the late medieval *Gottesfreunde* ('Friends of God'), a circle of mystics under the influence of Meister Eckhardt (*ca.* 1260–1328) and especially his disciple Johannes Tauler (*ca.* 1300–*ca.* 1361), who had a profound influence on the young Martin Luther. *Trans.*

23. Wilhelm Boelsche, in his edition of *Der Cherubische Wandersmann*, 1905, p. lxiv f.; similarly Fritz Mauthner, *Der Atheismus und seine Geschichte im Abendland*, 3 vols., 1922, p. 190f.

24. Vol. 4 (1923), p. 372f.

25. 'Crush the infamous thing!' – the famous slogan used against religion by the French Enlightenment philosopher Voltaire. *Trans.*

26. The water monster in Greek mythology slain by Hercules in his 'second labour'. The beast had nine heads, and every time one of them was cut off two more grew in its place. *Trans.*

3. THE TRUE RELIGION

1. Barth (following Paul) uses the Greek word *gnosis* ('knowledge'), which was the key term in the widespread movement in the Greco-Roman world known as Gnosticism. There were various kinds of Gnostics, some of whom wanted to interpret Jesus as the one who brings the secret Knowledge that will free the soul from its enslavement to this world of materiality and evil. *Trans.*

2. Barth puts this occurrence of his pivotal concept in quotation marks, apparently to signal that it is not being used in the dialectical sense developed in this section of the *Church Dogmatics*, but in one of its ordinary German senses. Here it carries only a negative meaning: these religious gifts will be annulled or suspended. *Trans.*

3. The terms *religio illicita* ('illicit religion') and *ecclesia pressa* ('persecuted church') refer to the official status and social position of the church in the Roman Empire before it became officially Christian in the fourth century. *Trans.*

4. The *corpus christianum* ('Christian body') expressed the ideal of the whole culture as one Christian community united under the church. *Trans.*

5. The idea of the maturity (*Mündigkeit*) of the modern age was subsequently developed by Dietrich Bonhoeffer in his prison letters and attracted considerable theological attention in the years following World War II. See Garrett Green, 'Modern Culture Comes of Age: Hamann versus Kant on the Root Metaphor of Enlightenment', in *What Is Enlightenment? Eighteenth-Century Answers and Twentieth-Century Questions*, ed. James Schmidt (Berkeley and Los Angeles: University of California Press, 1996), 291–305. *Trans.*

6. 'Justification of the ungodly [or impious]'. *Trans.*

7. See for the following: K. Florenz, 'Die Japaner', in Chantepie de la Saussaye, *Lehrb. d. Rel.-Gesch.*, 2nd ed., vol. 1, 1925, pp. 382ff., and Tiele-Söderblom, *Komp. d. Rel.-Gesch.*, 6th ed., pp. 197ff.

8. The Assyrian Church of the East, sometimes called 'Nestorian' in the West, split from the Byzantine Church of the West during the Nestorian schism in the fifth century; they sent missionaries to central and southern Asia in the seventh and eighth centuries. *Trans.*

9. 'Continuous creation'. *Trans.*

10. The medieval controversy between Nominalists and Realists concerned the relation of general concepts, or Universals, to particular things. Whereas the Realists maintained that Universals are real, the Nominalists argued that they are mere names (*nomina*; singular, *nomen*) and that only Individuals, or particular things, are real. *Trans.*

11. Barth is here describing the christological doctrine known as the Hypostatic Union, which received its classical formulation at the Council of Chalcedon in 451. According to Chalcedonian christology, the two natures, divine and human, of the incarnate *Logos* (Word), or Son of God, are united in the one *hypostasis*, or person, known as Jesus Christ. *Trans.*

12. Here Barth proposes that there is a 'continuous election' on the analogy of the familiar doctrine of a 'continuous creation' (see note 9 above). *Trans.*

13. Since Barth here explicitly appeals to Luther's translation, I have employed the King James Version in English, which is closer to Luther in both style and diction than are most modern translations, and which stands as the classic translation in English, just as does Luther's in German. *Trans.*
14. Here Barth plays deliberately on the fact that the verb *erwählen*, like 'elect' in English, can be used both doctrinally and politically. *Trans.*
15. 'Benefits of Christ'. *Trans.*
16. Hermann Samuel Reimarus (1694–1768), known from the posthumous *Wolfenbüttel Fragments* published by Lessing, was a deist who denied the miracles attributed to Jesus; he is commonly regarded as the founder of the modern historical critical study of the Bible. David Friedrich Strauss (1808–1874) wrote *The Life of Jesus Critically Examined*, one of the most controversial works of the nineteenth century, in which he tried to separate the 'historical Jesus' from the mythological accounts of the New Testament. Arthur Drews (1865–1935) denied the historicity of Jesus altogether, arguing that the New Testament account was purely mythological. *Trans.*
17. Barth's coinage to designate what he thinks is the Jesus-idolatry of eighteenth-century Pietism. *Trans.*
18. Barth, though he does not give the reference explicitly, is clearly citing John 6:68 in Luther's translation, which reads, 'Herr, wohin sollen wir gehen?' ('Lord, whither should we go?'). The Greek text, and most English translations, read, 'Lord, to whom should we go?' The difference, however, would not appear to affect Barth's point, which depends primarily on the following sentence (the same in all versions): 'You have the words of eternal life.' *Trans.*
19. See note 10 above. *Trans.*
20. An allusion to Amos 4:11. *Trans.*
21. Barth is following Luther's translation here, which reads, 'sind wir voll großer Freudigkeit' ('we are filled with great joyfulness'), but most modern versions translate, 'we are very bold' or something similar. *Trans.*

Select Bibliography

Bloesch, Donald G., *Jesus Is Victor! Karl Barth's Doctrine of Salvation* (Nashville: Abingdon, 1976).

Busch, Eberhard, *Karl Barth: His Life from Letters and Autobiographical Texts* (Philadelphia: Fortress Press, 2nd rev. edn, 1976).

Ford, David, *Barth and God's Story: Biblical Narrative and the Theological Method of Karl Barth in the 'Church Dogmatics'* (Studies in the Intercultural History of Christianity, 27; Frankfurt am Main: Lang, 2nd edn, 1985).

Gunton, Colin E., *Becoming and Being: The Doctrine of God in Charles Hartshorne and Karl Barth* (Oxford Theological Monographs, New York: Oxford University Press, 1978).

Hunsinger, George, *How To Read Karl Barth: The Shape of His Theology* (New York: Oxford University Press, 1991).

Jenson, Robert W., 'Karl Barth', in David Ford (ed.), *The Modern Theologians: An Introduction to Christian Theology in the Twentieth Century* (Cambridge, MA: Blackwell, 2nd edn, 1997).

Jüngel, Eberhard, *Karl Barth, a Theological Legacy* (Garrett E. Paul (trans.); Philadelphia: Westminster Press, 1st American edn, 1986).

Mangina, Joseph L., *Karl Barth: Theologian of Christian Witness* (Louisville, KY: Westminster John Knox Press, 2004).

McCormack, Bruce L., *Karl Barth's Critically Realistic Dialectical Theology: Its Genesis and Development, 1909–1936* (Oxford; New York: Clarendon Press; Oxford University Press, 1995).

Roberts, Tyler, 'Exposure and Explanation: On the New Protectionism in the Study of Religion', *Journal of the American Academy of Religion* 72 (2004), pp. 143–72.

Sykes, Stephen, *Karl Barth, Studies of His Theological Method* (Oxford; New York: Clarendon Press; Oxford University Press, 1979).

Torrance, Thomas Forsyth, *Karl Barth, Biblical and Evangelical Theologian* (Edinburgh: T&T Clark, 1990).

von Balthasar, Hans Urs, and Edward T. Oakes, *The Theology of Karl Barth: Exposition and Interpretation* (San Francisco: Communio Books, Ignatius Press, 1992).

Webb, Stephen H., *Re-Figuring Theology: The Rhetoric of Karl Barth* (SUNY Series in Rhetoric and Theology; Albany, NY: State University of New York Press, 1991).

Webster, J. B., *Barth* (Outstanding Christian Thinkers; London; New York: Continuum, 2000).

—— (ed.), *The Cambridge Companion to Karl Barth* (Cambridge Companions to Religion; Cambridge; New York: Cambridge University Press, 2000).